Word
Power

Word Power

A Writer's Guide

David L. Brown

Whether you want to write a short story,
a memoir, or even the Great American Novel,
this book will help you do it better.

MoabBookWorks

A Small Press for a Small World

www.moabbookworks.com

Introduction

Writing About Writing

To become a talented and accomplished writer is a worthy goal. The fact that you are holding this book in your hands or reading it on a screen indicates that you would seek to improve your ability to use words effectively.

The written word is arguably the most important, most influential, most dynamic discovery of human history. With the advent of writing, precious knowledge was no longer subject to the limits and failings of memory. Through the power of writing information could be recorded for all time, laws codified, great speeches preserved, poetry laid down like vintage wine for the enjoyment of generations far in the future.

In today's world we take the use of the written word almost for granted. Besides providing a record of knowledge it has become a medium of entertainment, through novels, short stories, memoirs and even plays and screenplays to be brought to life by actors.

There are many ways to craft powerful writing, writing that entertains, engages, informs and excites the reader. In the end you must find your own voice as a writer and this book can start you on that quest.

Understand that there is no single "right" way to write and in fact an almost infinite array of alternatives. Some are better than others; some are downright awful; a few rise to the heights of excellence. I'll help you learn to recognize the difference and hone your personal writing skills.

Note that this book focuses on the writing of fiction and memoirs – the use of narrative, dialog, scene descriptions and plotting drawn more from imagination than fact.

Non-fiction, which delivers facts or opinions (or at least should), requires somewhat different writing skills, although in some forms such as biographies it may also share some qualities of fiction. Think of the differences between a book of history and a historical novel. This book itself is, of course, an example of non-fiction.

Before we proceed, here's an important caveat: To become an excellent writer is no easy challenge. Psychologists have discovered something called the ten thousand hour rule. According to this, to achieve mastery of any complex skill requires ten thousand hours of practice. This has been shown for music, painting, brain surgery, competitive sports and many other non-trivial skills.

In the case of writing it's my belief that one needs to put in those ten thousand hours in both reading and writing. If you have not read widely you lack the foundation to write. That may sound like a lot of reading but for a dedicated reader who loves to write it's not that hard to achieve.

And of course not every violinist must strive to become concert master at the New York Philharmonic. You can work on improving your skills at every stage along the way and in fact it is essential that you do. No matter what your starting point this book is intended to help you move up to the next step.

You may wonder through what excess of pride and hubris I deem myself worthy to advise you on the art of writing. In all modesty I offer the fruits of my experience and study with no guarantee other than a promise to inform and enlighten you from my own knowledge gained through a lifetime as a writer and editor.

I am a non-recovering addict to the written word. I taught myself to read before entering school. When others were still struggling with *Nancy Drew* and the *Hardy Boys*, I was reading such books as *Moby Dick* and *Life on the Mississippi*. I edited a small town daily newspaper at the age of 19 and earned a degree from the top-rated Missouri School of Journalism at 20.

I have worked as newspaper reporter and columnist; magazine writer and editor; freelance photographer; writing coach; public relations consultant; blogger; and author of thousands of articles and more than half a dozen books including four novels.

My recent novel *Retirement Man* was awarded first prize in the mystery, suspense, thrillers and adventure category in an international competition, selected by the executive editor of Penguin Books.

I've worked as a freelance writer and photographer in more than 25 countries in Europe and the Far East.

I've served in leadership roles, most recently from 2008-2011 as vice-president and president of the Rio Grande chapter of the Society of Professional Journalists (New Mexico and West Texas).

I was named 2010 Citizen Journalist of the Year for SPJ's Region 9 (Utah, Wyoming, Colorado and New Mexico).

For two decades I owned a communications agency in Chicago that specialized in editorial stories for magazines and other written forms of communication. During that time I hired, trained and managed a couple dozen staff journalists and edited their output. My agency produced company magazines, newsletters, audio-visual programs, speeches, product literature and publicity articles, picking up numerous awards along the way.

In sum, I've put in my ten thousand hours as reader, writer, and editor several times over, but in the interest of full disclosure I am not a famous and highly paid writer. True, in 1979 I received $35,000 for writing a non-fiction book for a corporate client (in those days you could buy five average new cars or a couple of Mercedes-Benzes with that kind of cash) and I've written thousands of articles and other pieces of journalism and other commercial writing.

My more recent work, novels and non-fiction books, have been self-published for my own satisfaction to little notice and scant acclaim save for a small circle of devoted readers. Take that as you will. If you want to read a book about writing by Robert Ludlum, Norman Mailer, Truman Capote or Tom Clancy, you'll have a long wait. Sadly, relatively few famous authors have written books about their art. I'm here for you now, eager to share what I've learned in my half century as a writer and editor.

What will you learn from this book? Well, let's start with some things that you will *not* find in these pages:

• You will not read much about grammar because you should have mastered that in grade school (there's a reason why they called it "grammar school") and from extensive reading (and as noted above, no one who is not a reader can expect to become a writer of any note).

• You will not be lectured about hard-and-fast rules such as "never end a sentence with a preposition," because that's something I won't put up with. Rules should be learned as foundational knowledge, but once learned they are yours to break.

• Similarly, you will not be harassed about the use of infinitives (the basic forms of verbs, such as "to walk," "to go," "to sing," and so forth). The "rules" say you should never split an infinitive, but I say with tongue in cheek "try not to ever split an infinitive," a statement that falsifies itself. In fact, split infinitives often have better flow and are completely acceptable. Listen as William Shatner says, "to boldly go," and do likewise.

• You will not be instructed on how to diagram sentences. If a sentence makes sense, that's all you need to know. Not every sentence needs to be weighed down with enough subjects, objects, verbs, adjectives and general verbiage to break a mule's back. Four words may do. Sometimes two. But other times sentences can contain hundreds of words.

• You will not be warned never t'use contractions. They are natural and reflect the way people speak. When it meets your needs, writing should mirror the spoken word in all its many varieties. Make your characters speak like real people: write your passages much as you or your fictional characters might speak them. (Keep in mind that we are talking about the art of fiction here; in non-fiction, and particularly that of the academic kind, other rules apply.)

• Similarly, you will not be advised to shun "forbidden" words such as ain't and y'all or to avoid using common street language. As a writer you must expand the palette of your tools and how you use them – and the most familiar words can be the most powerful.

• Neither will you be advised to use big, expensive words just to impress people – but you will also be informed that very small words are as often as not inadequate to the task of fully expressing your intention. Although English offers many variations, there is usually one particular word that best meets your need. While keeping your readers in mind, that is the one that you should use.

What I will do is share with you a lot of thoughts and ideas from a lifetime of reading, writing and editing, including examples, advice from other writers and anecdotes to illustrate my points. We'll explore subjects such as these:

• How such disparate writers as Hemingway and Faulkner used words in their own special ways and how you can find your own voice as a writer.

• How you can make scenes come to life by activating all five of the reader's senses. After all, we do not experience the world around us merely by the power of sight. Let your readers taste the wine, smell the flowers, feel the gravel beneath their feet and hear the wind whispering in the trees.

• We'll explore the importance of choosing your words for their maximum effect, using my metaphorical "word target" which maps the most used words in the bull's-eye and with supporting words arranged in outlying circles.

• You'll discover how to attune yourself to the rhythm of your writing, crafting your stories almost as if they are blank verse poems or plays meant to be spoken aloud. A pleasing rhythm to your words is like well-laid brickwork to a garden wall. When your words are scattered around like stumbling blocks readers are sure to trip over them and will likely decide to invest their reading time elsewhere.

• We'll explore ways to make dialog sound "real." This is critical because dialog is the true backbone of any story, that thing that makes it get up and put on its boots. When its characters sound awkward and unnatural, no story can stand up and walk.

(Note: I favor the shortened version of the word over the British spelling "dialogue" so often seen.)

• You'll be introduced to the many reasons why you might want to avoid telling your story in the past tense as if it were a fairy tale from "once upon a time." Let the action roll like a movie in the present tense, then use the past tense for flashbacks.

• You'll see how important it is to keep antecedents and timelines in proper order to avoid confusing your readers. It's frustrating to read about an action that has become disconnected from its subject – did the butler say that or was it the chambermaid? Did the dog bark shortly after midnight, or was it when cocktails were being served on the veranda? These are little things that can make a big difference.

• You'll learn how to draw upon the wisdom and experience of others by using them as "beta readers" and sources of information. (No, not your mother; she loves you too much to be objective about your precious writing. No matter that it stinks like a week-old fish, she will praise your work to the skies.)

• Finally, you'll learn that although you can't count on breaking into the dying publishing industry unless your name is James Patterson or the zombie Robert Ludlum, there is a whole new world of self-publishing that may not make you rich but will give you a path to sharing your work with an audience of appreciative readers. You'll learn how to become a do-it-yourself publisher. It used to be said that power resides with the person who owns a printing press. These days we all can have that power.

• The subject of writing is almost without limits, so I'll include references and suggestions for further reading, including the counsel of many great writers in whose shadows I humbly stand.

• Finally, never forget that storytelling is serious business. Writing that is true and skillfully crafted with words of power can do far more than entertain – it can make your reader feel and in some cases actually change by absorbing the insights and philosophical truths that reside in your story.

Like legendary sorcerers or magi, the master storyteller can wield great power through those little things we call words. If you attain that skill you will make your reader smile with amusement, laugh, cry, cringe in terror, feel a tingle up their spine, be compelled to share your story with others, or blurt out a resounding Yes! when your protagonist survives to live another day.

Welcome to my world, a kind of workshop of the mind where words are tools through which thoughts, dreams, aspirations and imagination are brought to life thanks to that greatest of all human achievements – writing.

And when you want to come back for more, just click over to my website at www.moabbookworks.com where I'll continue to share my ideas and thoughts on the art and craft of the written word. I can help you with your own story, book, or memoir, too, with coaching and editing, and even provide self-publishing services through my imprint, Moab BookWorks. You may want to sign up for one of my writing workshops in Moab, Utah, or come for personal instruction. I'll be glad to show you this beautiful red-rock country while helping you wrestle with those pesky, slippery words.

Chapter 1

The Tools of a Writer

Writing in its most basic form is the ability to imitate sounds or speech through the use of symbols. These symbols are called words and they are the basic building blocks of all writing.

The mere ability to write or type words does not suffice to create writing that is "good" – that is, acceptably literate for everyday purposes. However, there are perhaps more than a billion people on earth today who can create writing in English that is "good" or close enough to get by.

From there it's a long step up to writing that is excellent, outstanding or superb. It could be compared to the difference between picking out "Chopsticks" on the piano and performing at Carnegie Hall to rave reviews.

The craft of writing all starts with words, those humdrum, everyday symbols that allow us to replicate the universe, whether as perceived or only imagined, on a page of text. In the hands of a master words are power, weapons of mass instruction. They yield the ability to influence others, share ideas, entertain and inform. Words can be woven into many patterns and like magical incantations or devout prayers they can allow your deepest inner thoughts and imaginings to shine forth.

The art of using words to create superior writing is the focus of this book. An important first step on this intellectual journey is to consider that most basic question: What are words and why are they important?

Words evolved through the ages in lockstep with humankind. Perhaps more than any other factor it is the mastery of language that sets us apart from the animal world. But words are slippery things. We often hear statements such as "those are only words" and it's true that language can be used to deceive as well as to shine the light of truth. For example, in formal debate each side uses similar words to present completely opposite views.

Words in themselves are merely tags to identify certain objects, ideas, actions or characteristics. As any pet owner knows, even animals use words.

Cats, for example, have a limited but easily recognized vocabulary of sounds for different purposes. The plaintive meow that demands food is quite different from the satisfied drone that invites you to scratch its ears.

There is no doubt that those sounds are primitive proto-words. Other animals have even more finely developed vocabularies — the growling, barking or baying of a wolf; the chattering of a monkey to tell when food has been found or to warn of danger; the mysterious and complex songs of whales. These simple animal vocabularies are audible "words." They are the substrate upon which our ancient ancestors built complex languages through millions of long dusty years.

Scientists hypothesize that the development of complex language was a key to the evolution and advancement of the human race. As a cooperative species rising from its animal past to create Stone Age societies our earliest forebears needed to process and share increasingly complex information. Making fire or shaping tools from flint demanded enhanced communication skills, lest the hard-gained knowledge of innovators be lost upon their deaths. How well could an innovator teach if deprived of the ability to communicate his or her hard-earned knowledge? To not only show, but to explain.

The pre-human creatures we call *Homo erectus* may have been the first to use fire and work flint, so it's fair to assume that they already had a command of words superior to that of lesser animals. Later Neanderthals and finally our more recent ancestors the Cro-Magnon must have built an ever-growing vocabulary of words to create and maintain increasingly complex lifestyles.

The myth of the Tower of Babel implies that there was once a tongue common to all humans and it may be true that the most primitive human languages, like those of many animals today, may have been shared in common. But as language moved beyond the most basic forms and humans spread across the earth, language evolved in different directions. Just as birds of unrelated tribes sing different songs, isolated human societies developed their own special grammars and vocabularies.

The power of words helped our ancestors to progress, step by steady step. And yet there was a strict restraint — the limits of human memory. Even the most incisive mind can remember only so much, and when that knowledge is passed on to successive generations only through speech there's always leakage. In the passage of time, facts become the stuff of fables; ideas blur and merge; names and places morph from everyday reality into myth.

Words are powerful but time is long and memory is frail.

And then, after hundreds of thousands of years, an incredible breakthrough occurred. To hijack a phrase from the *Book of John*, the word was made flesh.

We do not know the name of the man or woman who first learned to record words as symbols on stone, clay, papyrus or leather, but the inventors of fire and the wheel should stand in awe before the greatest unsung genius of them all, that unknown person who learned that words could be more than merely sounds from the mouths of speakers; that they could be recorded and passed down through the ages in undiminished form for as long as the language continued to exist.

From symbols that could be directly communicated only within the range of hearing and recalled only through fading memory sprang something powerful and transformative – Writing.

Just as the tongues of liars can betray, so can the written word. Thus have countless conquerors written one-sided histories; many a would-be hero placed themselves on pedestals of glory; and untold numbers of lies been fabricated to mislead and defraud. There is nothing pure or sacred about the written word for words are only the expressions of imperfect human beings.

Words are merely tools.

Nevertheless, they are of immeasurable importance. In tangible written form they are the solid bricks from which our ancestors built great civilizations. They remain the foundation stones of our world today.

As with all things words are sometimes used for good, sometimes for evil. Too often they are merely wasted in mindless drivel. But without them in what a poor and primitive state we humans would exist.

Words are of particular importance to you as an aspiring writer because they are the tools you will use to create writing that is more than merely "good." We are extraordinarily fortunate to work in the language we call English. It contains by far the most versatile, richest, delightful selection of words of any language on earth. Need a word for a particular meaning? English has it and usually a whole vocabulary list of words from which to choose.

In many respects English is not truly a language in and of itself but what is called a "borrowing" language, made up like a crazy quilt of words and grammar from many other languages, including Latin, German, Anglo-Saxon, Greek, Norse, Dutch, Celtic, French and many others. England was the original melting pot and its many cultural influences left us with the rich and varied language we know today.

It can be a bit overwhelming, actually, because there are so many choices. But one thing is clear – to attain power as a writer you must have a broad knowledge of English vocabulary. In short, to be a writer you must first a reader be.

There is a strong connection between writing and reading and to my mind it's not a chicken-or-egg thing. The ability to read clearly and well is a necessary prelude to good writing. It must come first.

As we enter the adventure we call life our brains are unformed vessels waiting to be filled, *tabula rasa* as the more pretentious among us like to say. (That's Latin for "blank slate" and it's a good example of metaphor, something we'll examine in detail in a later chapter.)

Think of those empty minds as like hard drives. We can choose to fill them with whatever we want, from meaningless word salad to rap music to pornography. Or we can cram them with ever more complex knowledge about the world and how things work.

And how do we fill those empty spaces in our heads with useful content? By listening to a self-appointed teacher drone on about something we could care less about? By comparing opinions with others whose heads are equally vacuous? Through some kind of magical osmosis in which we sit on a couch watching the Cartoon Channel? Hanging with the boys in the 'hood?

Well, no, I suggest that the real answer is that if our brains are to be supplied with useful stuff it will be through reading, and I don't mean comic books but quality pieces of writing. GIGO as the IT folks like to say: Garbage in, garbage out.

Think of it like this: As an individual you're surrounded by a small number of influencers including your parents, your siblings, your teachers, classmates and friends. It's a very small slice of a very large world. But through the power of words and those things called books (and now the Internet) you can connect with the entire universe of human knowledge, speculation, imagination and insight.

No person who has failed to master and exercise the art of reading can expect to produce clear, analytical writing. It follows as night after day that the ability to read and understand is the key to being able to produce writing that rises above the merely good. Those who fill their heads with junk can't be expected to craft stately sentences resonating with insight and wisdom.

And reading is a lot more than just being able to recognize letters and words. It's the connections between words that are important: the flow of the words in their total effect; the ideas and concepts that the words portray; the meaning of the darned things. Words are only the bricks and mortar from which phrases, sentences, paragraphs, chapters and entire books are built. Look at it from the point of view of the architect, not the guy who carries the bricks. Like anything else of importance reading really well requires practice and a lot of it. The challenge is to build a large and versatile vocabulary of words that you will later need as you aspire to become a masterful writer.

The late British writer Sir Terry Pratchett once said "to write, you must read extensively, both inside and outside your chosen genre and to the point of 'overflow'." He added that writers must "make grammar, punctuation and spelling a part of your life." I think what he meant was that the tools of language must be internalized so that their use comes naturally.

There is a related and much-ignored art that was once taught alongside reading and writing. It's called *diction* and it's all about how words are used to communicate clearly. Diction refers to the way an actor or orator uses language, including word choices, order and verbal emphasis, and the same principles can be applied to writing.

One of the best ways I know to judge a piece of writing is to read it aloud, and I don't mean in a monotone. Read the piece as an orator or actor might do it. When you hear the words you can get a better feel for how they're working together. In speaking as well as in writing the flow of the words matters. To become an excellent writer you must learn to recognize these patterns and how to craft sentences that flow easily from the tongue. Only then will they be pleasing to the eye.

Reading aloud is also a good way to improve reading skills. Remember that the written word is a relatively recent arrival in history. It's nothing more than an often-imperfect method of recording speech. Speaking, reading and writing are the great triad of human communication. Each is related to the other and none can stand alone for they are merely different aspects of the same thing, made of the same stuff, those things we call words.

There is a Swedish proverb that helps explain my point: "In a good book, the best is between the lines."

Now understand that I'm not recommending that you read books to learn how to write them (present and similar examples excepted). You should read for pure enjoyment and to satisfy your curiosity – but be aware that as you do your unconscious mind is busy squirreling away useful information about how words are used. Reading good writing is how we program our brains to make us good writers.

Chances are at this stage in your life, having picked up this book and hoping to become a more skillful writer, you likely have already put in your ten thousand hours of reading or at least are well on the way. It's a process that should have begun at a very early age and will continue as long as you live. We writers need to be emotionally involved with our craft. We need to love the written word and need to fill our minds with it just as we need to breathe the air.

Does it matter what you read? Well of course. It will do you little good to spend ten thousand hours reading comics or romance novels. Read what you like, of course, for entertainment and enlightenment. Even the occasional "bad" book provides a good learning experience, by clearly demonstrating things you shouldn't do as a writer.

Even if you have not already done so, I suggest reading some of the classics, works by such as William Faulkner, Ernest Hemingway, Charles Dickens, Jane Austin and Joseph Conrad, to name a few. Read poetry, too, especially by greats such as Alfred Lord Tennyson, William Wordsworth, Emily Dickinson, T. S. Eliot and Robert Frost. In a later chapter we'll see how the rhythm and flow of poetry can enhance your writing.

And read all the stuff that entertains you from among contemporary writers, and not just the "coming of age" novels that are popular among some, but also thrillers, mysteries and fantasy by such as Tom Clancy, Stephen King, Robert Ludlum and Terry Pratchett. Read non-fiction on subjects you enjoy, by writers such as Stephen Hawking, Richard Dawkins, Carl Sagan and Richard Feynman. By all means read the Harry Potter books and that marvelous *Lord of the Rings* trilogy. Read the *Holy Bible*, King James Edition, the grand chronicle from the early days of writing in emerging modern English.

All that reading is essential to learning to be a writer of quality because it provides the deep foundations on which the writer's skills are based.

Unfortunately, many people travel through life without ever priming their inner minds with serious reading. Among the unprepared, that thing some would-be writers call "writer's block" is usually due to the fundamental lack of proper preparation through insufficient reading and writing.

Before we move on, let me climb up on this handy soapbox to make an important announcement. Do I have your attention? Good, because this is something you need to know: *Just because you can benefit from reading classics doesn't mean you should attempt to write like them.* There is much to learn from the masters, but contemporary style is an ever-changing thing. No more than you would want to write in the style of *The Canterbury Tales* or *Pilgrim's Progress*, neither should you affect the style of even recent writers from the Twentieth Century such as Faulkner, Hemingway, or Steinbeck. Always strive to be contemporary, even when bending or breaking the rules. Choose to be ahead of the pack, not trailing behind like the guy at the end of the circus parade with the big broom and shovel

Let's take a close look at those tools, the words you'll use to craft your writing. It's estimated that there are as many as six hundred thousand to one million words in the English language. Now, certainly you don't want to use them all. Not even comprehensive dictionaries list nearly that many words. Many are specialized technical terms; others are obsolete or dated.

Most people for whom English is the primary language are familiar with around eight to ten thousand words. The typical educated reader is familiar with thirty or forty thousand. Shakespeare wrote all his plays and sonnets using about thirty thousand words, nearly two thousand of which he coined himself.

Now it may seem a bit daunting to have to deal with so many words. A carpenter would throw up his hands if he had to use thousands of different tools. That may help explain why it takes at least ten thousand hours of reading to build a sufficient vocabulary on which to build advanced writing skills. Of course, nobody actually uses forty thousand words in everyday life. It's estimated that knowing about three thousand is sufficient to understand ninety-five percent of everyday writing or speech.

It's important to realize that not every potential reader shares your vocabulary. The more unfamiliar words you use, the more readers you'll lose. You must control your urge to use that fancy term you just heard spouted by some posturing pundit on C-SPAN 3. Chances are if you didn't know that word before, few of your readers will know it either.

I like to think of words as arranged on a palette shaped like a target, with a bull's eye and several concentric rings. In the center are those words that are most often used: the three thousand or so that any moderately literate person may use or encounter every day.

In the first ring around the bull's eye are those words that round out the vocabulary of the average person, eight to ten thousand common words that are familiar to most English readers.

In the second ring are those additional words known to more educated readers, the balance of the thirty to forty thousand words that are familiar to those having a good grasp of the language although not in everyday use.

Finally, the rest of the words of the English language are relegated to the outer rings of the language target like far-distant comets in the mysterious Oort Cloud that surrounds our solar system.

Keeping that image in mind, let's consider how to apply this information to use words effectively. It's obvious that you should use as many words as possible from near the center of the target and be very cautious about using words that fall further out. Take note that your perceptions may vary about exactly where a certain word falls on the language target. You must learn to use your own judgment about which words are best to use for your audience. Here's one caveat: Those with limited vocabulary are not likely to be readers, so it's pointless to lower the threshold in hopes of luring them into your story. To put it another way, J.K. Rowling explains: "Books are like mirrors: if a fool looks in, you cannot expect a genius to look out."

In general terms, it's reasonable to say that seventy to eighty-five percent or more of the words you use should come from the bull's eye of the target, those three thousand or so most common.

Most of the rest should come from the first ring containing eight to ten thousand common words plus a scarce few from the second ring with its thirty to forty thousand words known to but not necessarily commonly used by educated readers.

This is only a seat-of-the-pants estimate and should be adjusted with an eye to your audience. When writing juvenile fiction, stay closer to the bull's eye

It's said that Dr. Seuss used only 225 words to write *The Cat in the Hat* and that on a bet with his publisher he wrote *Green Eggs and Ham* using only 50. Of course, his readers were young children with very limited vocabularies. If you're writing a sophisticated novel for the Beautiful People, let more of the first and second ring words flow through your fingertips.

As far as the rest of the vast English language, proceed with extreme caution. Of course, there are times when specialized jargon, technical terms or other unfamiliar words must be used because they are essential to the story. In that case the word should be defined for the reader.

No, you shouldn't stop in the middle of a sentence and insert a dictionary definition. Defining can be slipped in without breaking the flow and can even help make the story interesting, perhaps something like this:

> "I'm concerned about your (insert unfamiliar medical term here)," the doctor says, frowning at Bob's chart.
>
> "What's that?" Bob asks in alarm. "Oh my God, is it serious?"
>
> "Oh, I hardly think so," the doctor replies with a chuckle. "It's only (define term in simple everyday words).

Thus you can make your characters explain unfamiliar words to your readers, such as through the doctor's reply to Bob. This will inform your readers and leave them thinking they're a bit smarter for having read your passage. Had you just thrown the term around without explanation they would probably have an opposite reaction. Of course, you don't want to use a term like this unless there's a reason, such as if that unfamiliar medical term is to become pertinent to Bob's experience as the story unwinds.

There is software that can help you determine the readability of your work. Most commonly used are the Flesch Reading Ease Score and the Flesch-Kincaid Grade Level Score. Both are available on Microsoft Word™ and many other word processors.

The Reading Ease Score is based on a formula that analyzes the number of words per sentence (based on the assumption that longer sentences make for harder reading which may not be entirely true) and the average number of syllables per word. The score is on a scale of 1 to 100 and the suggested goal for most writing is a score between 60 and 70.

The Flesch-Kincaid Grade Level Score rates a piece of writing by the degree of education required of the reader. The goal here is for most writing for adults to aim for the seventh to eighth grade levels.

For demonstration, the part of this book that you've read so far scores about 62 on the Flesch Reading Ease Score and at the ninth grade level on the Flesch-Kincaid Grade Level Score. Note that even though I assume I'm writing to a fairly sophisticated audience these scores fall into or near the suggested ranges.

Now you can't rely too much on these readability tests because they are based on simple formulas that do not take into account such factors as how sentences are constructed, which actual words are used and so forth. One could imagine a piece of writing that scores well while being almost entirely incomprehensible. In fact, we see examples almost each day. As an exercise you might try to see if you can craft a piece that scores well and yet is made up entirely of gibberish.

In any event, I wouldn't take the reading scores too seriously and you probably shouldn't try to force your writing style to elicit a "good" reading score.

As I've mentioned, another way to judge your writing, one that I personally use, is to read the written piece aloud, either to yourself or to another. If your tongue stumbles over a sentence, chances are that revision is in order. Reading to someone else provides clues when the listener looks puzzled or stops you frequently to ask for explanations. Reading aloud also helps you sense the rhythm and flow of your writing, something we'll cover in a later chapter.

Before we leave this subject let's take a quick review of the types of word-crafting tools you'll be working with. Again, this is something you would have learned in grammar school but it pays to be reminded before we proceed. In English, words are categorized in eight generally recognized types.

Nouns are words that denote an abstract or concrete thing, such as a person, a place, or even an idea or quality, such as *happiness* or *courage.*

Pronouns are words that substitute for a noun, such as *they, her, it.* There are three categories of pronouns: Subject (*he*); Object (*him*); and Possessive (*his*). Pronouns must always have a clear antecedent, the noun to which they refer.

Nouns and pronouns are necessary, of course. They are to sentences like the bricks and timbers of a house. Other valuable tools are those that describe and amplify objects and actions. These can be compared to the doors, windows and furniture of the house, the things that make it pleasing to the eye and a place you would want to live. They must also be used with discretion and never without good purpose.

The first of those are called *Adjectives*, words that qualify or amplify a noun or pronoun; in other words, that describes them (example: *big*). Adjectives are among the most important tools in your writer's toolkit. Along with adverbs, they are sometimes called *modifiers*.

Of perhaps equal importance is the category known as *Verbs*. These are words that indicate action, movement, or a state of being (run, sit, be).

Just as adjectives describe nouns, *Adverbs* qualify or amplify adjectives or verbs (examples: *very big; run quickly*). Adverbs can often be recognized by ending in *–ly* or *-wise*, although this is not always so and some words ending in –ly are not adverbs.

Then there are the words that hold everything together, the nails and mortar to continue the building metaphor. These are *Prepositions, Conjunctions* and *Interjections.*

Prepositions are words that show the relationship between things, such as *at, on, behind, over.* The prepositions *of, to* and *in* are among the ten most often used words in English.

Conjunctions are words that connect other parts of a sentence, such as *for, and, but, or* and *so.*

Interjections are single words or short phrases that communicate an emotional reaction. They serve a function somewhat like those emoticons with smiley or frowny faces that are so common today in informal writing. They are often followed by an *exclamation* point. Examples are *hooray!*, *ouch!* and *damn!*.

Beware of verbs or adjectives that are transformed into nouns through the addition of suffixes such as *-ment, -ation, -ing*. This is called *nominalization*, which itself is an example of what it describes. Try to keep words in the right corrals, not mixing the calves with the sheep.

Writing in *The New York Times*, the Australian academic Helen Sword outlined the dangers of nominalization this way:

> Nouns formed from other parts of speech are called nominalizations. Academics love them; so do lawyers, bureaucrats and business writers. I call them "zombie nouns" because they cannibalize active verbs, suck the lifeblood from adjectives and substitute abstract entities for human beings:
>
> The proliferation of nominalizations in a discursive formation may be an indication of a tendency toward pomposity and abstraction.
>
> The sentence above contains no fewer than seven nominalizations, each formed from a verb or an adjective. Yet it fails to tell us who is doing what. When we eliminate or reanimate most of the zombie nouns (tendency becomes tend, abstraction becomes abstract) and add a human subject and some active verbs, the sentence springs back to life:
>
> Writers who overload their sentences with nominalizations tend to sound pompous and abstract.
>
> Only one zombie noun – the key word nominalizations – has been allowed to remain standing."

When you use a nominalization your sentence may become unclear, awkward or verbose. To fix it, identify the original verb and the actor using it and construct the sentence accordingly. Another term for this is *verbing*, and it's OK as long as it works, but when it creates a monstrosity such as "verbing," get out your crucifix, hammer and stake and go zombie hunting.

Of course, many nominalizations have become so well entrenched in the language that they're inescapable, nouns such as *writing, singing, wishes, building*, and so forth. You must use your judgment about when a nominalization requires your attention.

Here are some more suggestions:

• Be cautious about using the qualifier *very*, as it usually doesn't add to the qualities of the subject verb or adjective and can raise the question of just how true it is (examples: *very honest, very dark, very long, very bright*). Adding the word very doesn't make a person any more honest or a room any darker. Don't write: "she was very cold," when you can say: "she was freezing." Instead of "very big," choose "huge" or "immense" or some other appropriate word. Replace "very bright" with "brilliant," and so forth. Using such qualifiers as "very" is a sign the subject noun or verb is weak, so replace it instead of propping it up with another word.

Mark Twain once suggested that when tempted to use the word *very*, write instead *damn*, thus assuring that "your editor will remove it and all will be as it should be."

• Also avoid *illogical modifiers*, such as "really unique" and "perfectly clear". Adding a modifier doesn't make things any more unique or clear. However, although caution is advised, modifiers when used properly can enhance the rhythm and flow of your prose.

• Similarly, avoid using quotation marks simply to emphasize a word in your narrative. This is sometimes called grocer's punctuation, for amusing examples such as green "onions," fresh "eggs," and so forth. Quotation marks can imply the stated "fact" isn't true, just as in my use there. When you don't intend to bring facts into question, avoid quote marks and use italics or boldface to highlight words.

• Another annoying habit to avoid is *hedging* everything you say with dodgy words and phrases such as *about, nearly, possibly, in part, according to some* and so forth. I don't mean to say you shouldn't qualify a statement when required for clarity, but constant hedging quickly becomes tedious. It gets in the way of your story. Many things are not one hundred percent clear and whenever possible you should give the reader credit for knowing when uncertainty exists.

• This raises another point: Say what you have to say in the clearest way you can, then get on with the story. Don't be fixated on the fear of leaving your readers behind. It's their responsibility to keep up. If they can't, chances are they're not the readers you're looking for.

• Keep in mind that to become an excellent or even merely good writer is a lifelong endeavor. As in all things there's no such thing as perfection in writing, only the satisfaction of making steady progress toward the unobtainable goal.

• Good writing reflects those key human actions, speaking and seeing. The better it does so, the better the writing. Hemingway used to refer to writing that is true, and it's your challenge to craft words that are apt to strike the reader as reasonable descriptions of a possible world. Write words that are true and you will lead your readers on.

• It can help to create an image in your mind of a particular reader and write as if carrying on a conversation with him or her.

• Recognize that much of your writing comes from your unconscious mind. Stories come from the same places as our dreams, and in fact when we dream our unconscious minds are telling us stories. Listen to that mysterious part of your brain, for there is much wisdom there.

• Call things by their names, and use the simplest and most familiar. I once spent time in the Montana high country with a hunting guide who had a special name for almost everything. Eggs were "cackleberries," and when he wanted the Grey Poupon™ he asked me to "pass the mouse turd." It was amusing, but irritating at the same time. I remember challenging him, saying: "John, don't you ever call anything by its right name?" You can take a lesson from John's quirky diction. Don't call an earthquake "an earth shaking event," or a folding cot a "portable sleeping device." It's OK to call a spade a spade. Really.

• Excessive wordiness almost always weakens the power of your words. As mentioned above, when the need for an adjective or adverb appears, it may be a sign you've chosen a weak noun or verb. Instead of trying to patch it up with a modifier, look for a stronger word. Example: instead of *bright red*, write *scarlet*.

• Of course, modifiers have their place, so don't hesitate to use them when appropriate. However, it's a good idea to avoid using more than one. If you have two modifiers (example: a big, tall mountain), choose the strongest.

These guidelines are aimed at helping you craft sentences that are streamlined and flow easily. As always, reading them aloud is a good way to tell when your sentences are bogged down in a swamp of verbiage. Listen to your words. Yes, your writing has a sound and it can be musical and rhythmic or clanging and discordant. It is your voice as a writer and you want it to be clear and melodious.

Grammar is like a software app to process words into functional sentences. We learn to use this useful tool from about the age of two. Although grammar is an interesting subject, to be an excellent writer doesn't require you to learn the intricate details of grammar any more than you need to know the programming code for Microsoft Word™ in order to use it.

The rules of grammar are imposed after the fact, for as linguistics research has shown, it's hardwired in our brains. *Syntax* (word order) and *word formation* (throw, threw, throwing) are the elements of grammar. Once you learn, for example, that in English an article (*the*) precedes a noun (*ball*), you don't have to relearn it every time you refer to a different noun. It's programmed into your brain, which is the equipped mind of a writer.

For a proper understanding of our toolkit known as the English language, you should realize that languages are like living things – that which is considered "proper" changes from one generation to the next. Following are versions in English of the 23rd Psalm showing how the language changed over a millennium:

Old English (800-1066)
Drihten me raet, ne byth me nanes godes wan.
And he me geset on swythe good feohland.
And fedde me be waetera stathum.

Middle English (1100-1500)
Our Lord gouerneth me, and nothyng shal defailen to me.
In the sted of pastur he sett me ther.
He norissed me upon water of fyllyng.

King James Bible (1611)
The Lord is my shepherd, I shall not want.
He maketh me to lie down in green pastures.
He leadeth me beside the still waters.

Modern (1989)
The Lord is my shepherd, I lack nothing.
He lets me lie down in green pastures.
He leads me to still waters.

It's interesting to note that the language has not only changed, it's also become simpler, at least in these examples. There is a lesson in there, one that most "rules for writers" feature very prominently: Use words economically, using the simplest ones that will do the job and eliminating any that are not absolutely necessary.

As Ralph Waldo Emerson put it: "It is not enough to write so you can be understood; you must write so clearly that you cannot be misunderstood."

Karl Popper, reasonably considering perfection to be an impossible goal, put it slightly differently: "It is impossible to speak in such a way that you cannot be misunderstood." Obviously, as a writer you face a serious challenge in making your meaning clear.

Enough said about the taxonomy and evolution of words. As promised in the introduction, I'm not going to belabor rules of grammar. Let's get on with how to master the craft of writing.

Chapter 2

Preparing for the Journey

When you resolve to write a story, memoir or novel you are in essence proposing to embark on a journey of discovery. Like any journey, it pays to know where you are going and how you intend to get there.

So, how do we prepare for this journey of imagination, this difficult road on which we propose to travel? Well, I'm sorry to say there's no simple answer. First comes the need to determine the broad outline of how you'll approach the challenge.

For example, there are two completely different approaches to writing a novel. It's as if some writers are dogs and others are cats. One type, let's call them dogs, figure everything out in great detail before even beginning to write. He or she will write a long synopsis of the plot, invent the background of each character, set down a strict timeline of action and create lists of supporting information. The finished plan might almost comprise a book all in itself, perhaps fifty pages or more just to create a roadmap. An example is the novelist Ken Follett who prepares detailed outlines and background profiles before writing the first word.

Cats, on the other hand, start with a few general ideas about what the novel will be about and simply begin to write. Stephen King writes that way, as do many others. Somehow characters appear and events occur and it all works out as if by magic. I think cats actually do something similar to what dogs do, except that they do a lot of it in their heads and at least in part in their unconscious minds.

I know in my own case that characters often do things that I never expected, and that is a thrilling experience. I could not be a dog because if I knew exactly how a novel would proceed it would take the fun out of the adventure of creating it.

Here is an explanation from another cat writer, the late Robert Ruark, from his autobiographical novel *The Honey Badger*:

> In the working life of a professional author, if he is lucky, the fictional characters take over and become fleshly people, with solid dimensions and minds of their own. They do things the author never intended. They say things the author never dreamed of. The happy author is thus reduced to the minor role of coachman, using no whip, driving only with a very slack rein.

In a note to his novel *The Tragedy of Puddn'head Wilson*, Mark Twain describes how he envisioned several characters before beginning to write, only to see them overshadowed by new and more interesting characters that appeared on the scene unbidden. He jokes that he considered having the original characters all walk out their back doors, fall into wells and drown. In the end he left them in as very minor characters.

Deciding whether you are a dog or a cat depends upon which way works best for you. It may be a left-brain, right-brain thing. There is no right or wrong way. Each is valid, and in fact as I present them, they are opposite ends of a spectrum of alternatives. You may find a mid-point that works best for you, taking a bit from the dogs and some from the cats.

* * * * *

No matter which way you choose to work, there are certain things that you need to decide before you start. We can apply the old journalist's checklist of who, what, where, when and how. The first two are obvious: the "who" is you and the "what" is the story you have decided to tell. That leaves decisions to be made about *where* you will do the work; *when* you will do it; and *how* you will do it. Let's take those one at a time.

Writing is a solitary art. It's important to find the proper *where* for your working style. It's difficult or perhaps impossible for many of us to create fine writing amid the chaos of demanding children, blaring TV sets or rock music videos. Others are comfortable writing among distractions, at least up to a point. The young Ernest Hemingway used to write in Parisian cafes. Others must achieve a monk-like separation from every distraction. The serious writer must address this question of finding the workplace that allows his or her work to flow unimpeded.

In his book *On Writing*, Stephen King describes how he once converted a large room into a spacious home office, placing an enormous desk in the middle. The result: he recalls spending five years being drunk and sitting behind the desk. After he beat his drinking habit he got rid of the big desk and set up a smaller one against the wall in a remote corner and as far as I know has been writing there happily ever since.

Like King, some writers designate a special room at home in which to do their writing. Others may use a guesthouse or even rent a small private office nearby.

Whichever way you choose, you need to set up guidelines for yourself and others. The workspace should not contain anything to distract you from your work. No TVs. No enticing books other than reference material related to your work. No comfy chair or sofa for napping. No guest chair, because you do not want to encourage visitors. It's a good idea not to have a phone in your workspace, or at least to turn it off while working. If possible, choose a room with no window.

You might find that snuggling in your bed with a laptop or a college ruled notebook and a Bic™ is the perfect way for you. Or you may like to take your laptop or notebook down to the beach or to a quiet forest glade. Find the very special *where* that works for you.

I often work while listening to music played through my computer. I do not choose tracks with vocal parts, because spoken words intrude on my thoughts. Right now I'm listening to some Spanish guitar music.

Then there's that worst of all modern distractions, the Internet, constantly tempting us to check our email accounts or browse among an endless array of fascinating blogs and websites. I do use the Internet when writing, to do the all-important research required to find or double-check facts that help make stories seem real. It's a tremendous tool for a writer, but it takes a force of will to avoid constant web surfing or obsessive email checking.

One way to deal with that is to set a schedule for Internet use, say ten minutes set aside at the beginning of each hour. You need to take a break from time to time anyway and by relegating the distractions of the web to a defined period of time you can free up the other fifty minutes of each hour for your work. That might also be a good time to fix a fresh cup of tea or crack a bottle of water. Get up and stretch, walk around, maybe even go outside to make sure the world is still there. Then, when the ten minutes are up, get back to work. You might want to use a kitchen timer to remind you when it's time to take a break.

And here's another thing to consider: Many of the finest writers have had serious problems with alcohol and some believe that drinking helps stoke their creativity. Tennessee Williams, Jack

Kerouac, Dylan Thomas, John Cheever, Ernest Hemingway, F. Scott Fitzgerald, Jack London and many others were legendary drinkers.

Before swearing off booze, Steven King admits he wrote *Cujo* in a constant state of inebriation and has no memory of having done it.

Handle this aspect of your writing life as best suits your personality and needs. I like to have a drink at the end of the day, but since I write during the daytime I'm always cold sober when doing so. Well, almost always.

Although a renowned drinker, Hemingway must have understood the danger, as in *For Whom the Bell Tolls* he wrote of drink as "a deadly wheel" on which drunkards "ride until they die." He took his own life at age 61.

My experience of living and dealing with an alcoholic and now deceased wife taught me that there's no benefit from over-indulgence in liquor. I doubt that drinking is necessary for writing that is better than good, and I do not advise it – but if it helps you be a better writer, and if you can keep the demons at bay, I'm not going to stand in your way. It's your life to live and your stories to tell. And, by the way, the same applies to drugs of other kinds.

The next point, *when* you will do your work, is also of critical importance. If you wait for your muse to appear, chances are she never will. Set aside specific times to write. Ann Rice used to write late at night, churning out *Interview with the Vampire* in just five weeks by doing research during the day and most of the writing late at night while her husband slept.

As much as possible, plan your writing around specific times. You will need to provide for other phases of your life, such as time with family and the demands of your "day job" if you are for-tunate/unlucky enough to have one (they can really be a mixed blessing). Let your family, friends and co-workers know about your schedule and ask them not to call or visit during work periods. If you work at home and other family members are present, by all means close the door to your home office while working and demand that you not be disturbed.

Finally, choose the physical way you will create your writing, the *how*. Traditionally, writing was a pen-and-pencil art and many fine novels were written in longhand, even after typewriters became common. Typewriters were for secretaries, not writers, I guess. I recall seeing an advertisement for Ticonderoga pencils featuring Robert Ludlum, who claimed to have written his thrillers with the company's No. 2 pencils.

I suspect that more than a few writers still prefer to write by hand. However, in this post-modern world chances are you will use a computer and most probably you will use Microsoft Word™. Typing isn't just for secretaries any more.

You may prefer a laptop that you can carry around with you. My own choice is to use a machine with a large monitor. I'm writing this on a 27-inch iMac™. The oversized screen allows me to display my pages at 150 or 200 percent of actual size for easy reading and editing, and with space to open a web page to one side when doing research.

I use a large, humpbacked split keyboard that keeps my wrists in a comfortable position. I find that typing on the itsy-bitsy keyboards that come with most computers, and especially those built into laptops, is awkward and uncomfortable. You want to eliminate any such factors that will discourage you from writing.

Another option is to use speech recognition software such as Dragon™. This could be very efficient, although I have never tried it. I think one reason it doesn't appeal to me is that I tend to edit as I go. With speech transcription I would need to do all the revisions and edits later. I like to make changes when they're fresh in my mind. The way I work, when I finish a writing session I have a nearly complete draft of that section.

Here are some more details of my personal writing habits (I'm not prescribing them as a model, but only as examples). I tend to write in the mornings, then go back and edit and refine the day's output in the afternoon. I usually reserve the rest of the afternoons for chores and errands and evenings for my obsessive reading (often three or four books a week), or social activities.

Due to other obligations or interests I don't write all the time (as perhaps few other than James Patterson and Stephen King might), but when a book is coming into being I try to write at least nearly every day. When a story is telling itself it pays to pay attention, because otherwise it will grow stale and you'll likely lose interest. More important, the characters will lose interest in you and their story will go untold.

I generally try to complete a chapter during each session. For my novels I tend to write moderately long chapters, usually around 2000-2500 words. A finished novel of eighty to a hundred thousand words will thus contain around forty chapters, representing about forty active days of first draft writing. When the draft is done I spend another day or two going over the entire manuscript for a final edit and proofreading.

Unlike many writers I perform these necessary steps myself, having been an editor for some years and having developed an eye for proofreading by operating a commercial typesetting business as part of my communications agency.

Unless you are similarly qualified, I strongly recommend that you seek the services of an editor and/or proofreader to go over the final draft. We'll discuss these editing and production steps in a later chapter.

When I'm satisfied, I set the manuscript aside for a month or two to "age" before giving it a final read and polish.

Finally, let's look at that all-important subject of how to motivate yourself to actually produce the writing you've set out to create. When you're supposed to be traveling toward your destination, you don't want to sit on the side of the road watching the traffic go by.

Sometimes when I was running my communications agency in Chicago, one of my staff writers would tell me they just couldn't figure out how to get started on an assignment. They would sometimes mention something they called "writer's block."

I would inform them that there is no such thing. I sincerely believe that, and there is a simple way to get around those imagined blocks: Follow the advice of Nike™ and "just do it." I would tell the writers to simply start writing without trying to think up the best way to start. In every case, before long they would discover an appropriate beginning.

Remember my earlier remarks about writers that proceed with no specific plan, the ones I called cats? I suggested that a lot of their inspiration and reckoning might come from their unconscious minds. I think that's at work here, too. If you try to consciously think about just what words to put down you can freeze up while all along the right phrases may be lurking in your unconscious mind, waiting for you to start typing.

Think of it as kind of like an action sport: A baseball player who has to stop and think about how to hit the ball as it leaves the pitcher's hand at 90 m.p.h. is certain to fail miserably. He has to hone his batting skills through long practice and respond to the pitch by letting his prepared brain take care of things. There's no time to consciously think about it.

It's the same with many other ordinary actions. Once we've learned to walk or ride a bicycle, play the piano, eat spaghetti, jump rope, light a fire, avoid touching the resulting hot stove or myriad other things, we don't have to think about them again. Similarly, we're born with the innate knowledge of how to breathe and keep our hearts pumping blood. Our brains know what to do, and thank goodness we never have to remember to take a breath or keep our hearts beating.

It's kind of like that with writing. If your keyboard isn't clicking you're not writing, it's as simple as that. Get those ideas and words down on paper or on your monitor and sort them out later. The best part of this is that the more you write, the more natural it will become. Just as a ball player can create within his mind the ability to hit a fastball, you will be cultivating the brain of a writer.

I guess another way to express this idea is to say: "Don't just sit there, write!" It may not work for everyone, but it works for me and it worked for the staff writers I managed. You might even want to make up a little sign with those words and post it above your workspace.

An important goal should be to always finish what you start. The science fiction writer Robert Heinlein made this a main point of his five-point "Rules for Writing:"

1. You must write.
2. You must finish what you write.
3. You must refrain from rewriting,
    except to editorial order.
4. You must put the work on the market.
5. You must keep the work on the market
    until it is sold."

These suggestions were crafted for a commercial writer such as Heinlein was and may not apply in your case. His advice about rewriting doesn't apply to someone who is learning the craft, but you should know when to stop. You'll learn from working through challenges; little is gained if you quit when the going gets hard.

It's been said that writing is a craft, and that storytelling is an art. Your challenge as a writer of fiction is to master both. There are two doors to the mastery of writing: talent and skill. You may have to be born with the first, and I hope you were, but skills can and must be learned.

You must believe in yourself and honor your work at every stage. Writing can be a magical experience but talent alone is not enough – none of us emerge from the cradle equipped with the tools of an excellent writer.

Nobody can truthfully say that writing is easy. It can be darned hard, but like any piece of work the best approach is to just roll up your sleeves and get to it. In a very real sense there's only one person who can teach you to become an accomplished writer, and that person is you. Others can point the way and provide coaching tips, but it's on you to do the heavy lifting.

And as I end this chapter let me put on the shabby, metaphorical trench coat of fictional TV detective Lieutenant Columbo, turning at the door as if in afterthought to murmur, "Oh, there's just one more thing."

And here's that thing, a very important one indeed: What should you write about?

Ah! For a writer, that's the key question, isn't it?

It used to be common practice among critics and teachers to advise us in no uncertain terms to write about "what you know." I had a professor in a fiction writing class at the Missouri School of Journalism who believed that.

I submitted a short story about a guerilla fighter in an uprising in some eastern European nation. I was a 19-year-old kid who knew nothing of such things beyond having read Hemingway and Koestler and Dos Passos and Orwell and Faulkner. He gave me a C+ and wrote a comment about his belief in writing what you personally know. I was judged not for my writing, but for my life experience, or lack thereof.

Next time I decided to test his theory, but not by writing about what *I* knew but what I imagined *he* might know, or think he knew. His name was Tom MacAfee and he was from Alabama. He wrote and had published stories and a novel in the *genré* known as Southern Writing, all about rednecks and poverty, I suppose, and inbred hillbillies with receding chins and a crock of white lighting close at hand. For my next assignment I wrote a story about a Southern boy who encounters a gang of coon hunters in the woods.

I had never seen a raccoon in my life and knew about the South only from having read all of Faulkner and a few other authors, but I got a straight A for that story.

I had learned an important lesson, and the best I can state it it's that you can write from what you *know* at second hand as well as from personal experience. I wrote of that Southern boy from my imagination and indirect knowledge, and it seemed to my professor to be true because it resonated with what he knew about the world. I had experienced the South by reading the words of others.

Did Thomas Harris know the taste of human flesh when he wrote about Hannibal Lector?

Did Edgar Rice Burroughs swing from vines and hang out with a chimpanzee?

Did Isaac Asimov design robots and imbue them with the Three Laws of Robotics?

Well, yes they did – but in their creative minds, not in the mundane "real" world in which we all live, longing to escape to something more ... interesting.

Franz Kafka, known for his imaginative stories, wrote an entire book, *Amerika*, about a country that he had never visited.

Good fiction comes from our knowledge, but not in any direct way like water running from a tap. First it must be processed through our unconscious minds, honed and refined, made part of a matrix of secret knowledge that not even we ourselves can know or understand until it comes pouring out onto the page.

What should you write about? By all means, write based on what you know from your own experience, but also about that which you can imagine – and always with emphasis on the latter. The wonderful experience of creativity does not come from without but from within your prepared mind, the mind of a writer. Just sit down at the keyboard and if you have the heart and brain of a writer you will discover for yourself the magical fact that you are filled with stories that yearn to be told.

Chapter Three

Drawing On Your Inner Poet

Except in dictionaries, words are seldom found alone. They are not by nature solitary things but flock joyously together to make coherent phrases, sentences, paragraphs, and great works of literature. Just as glorious cathedrals can be created from unremarkable stones, mere words can be crafted into memorable chapters, books and entire libraries.

But just as the construction of a cathedral requires the skill and experience of master architects, masons and sculptors, to achieve a fine piece of writing demands a great deal of thought, skill and tenacity on the part of the writer. Words must not be thrown together helter-skelter. The art of the wordsmith is required to create writing that is dignified, pleasing to the eye and ear, and clearly expresses the intended message.

The choice of words and the order in which they are placed in a sentence make all the difference. There is a special correctness about a well-crafted sentence. When words flow smoothly together, their meaning is revealed with deceptive ease. A good sentence knows where it's going and makes it its business to get there while carrying along the mind of the reader.

It is always incumbent upon the writer to use a word that is "right" in the sense of meaning. But there is another way that words must be "right," and that is in how they fit into the rhythm and flow of the sentence of which they are part. A word can be absolutely correct as far as its meaning, but if it stands in the middle of a sentence like a concrete block on a busy freeway, it is nevertheless wrong. Just as in Frank Herbert's *Dune*, "the spice must flow," so it is with words.

Choosing an appropriate word does not necessarily create a challenge to the accomplished writer. Fortunately, English is the most versatile language in human history. It contains myriad words with meanings that are similar or exact, words with roots in Latin, Old Norse, Greek, Celtic, French and a melting pot of other languages.

If the first English word that comes to mind doesn't fit the flow, you can always try an alternative. Another solution is to rearrange the words around the offending one, making it fit into the rhythm.

Applying rhythm and flow to strings of words almost certainly began long ago in the days before the invention of writing. We know this from the way the poet Homer composed his heroic tales to be recited from memory by bards, traveling storytellers.

As addressed in an earlier chapter, human memory is frail, and writing had not yet been invented when Homer composed his masterworks. To help prevent the threads of his idylls from fraying and unwinding over time the great storyteller used two tricks to help lock in his meaning.

First, as we all remember from high school English, the words were strung together in a fixed pattern or rhythm. Homer's tales were told in a form known as dactylic hexameter. That form presents each line as six pairs of syllables. In English a more common form is iambic pentameter, a style in which there are five sets of syllables, so this is the form most translations have taken.

Here is an example as translated from *The Iliad*:

> Inflaming wine, pernicious to mankind,
> Unnerves the limbs, and dulls the noble mind.

The alternating rhythm of the pentameter is clear, as you can see when the emphasized syllables of the first line are placed in boldface: "Inflaming wine, pernicious to mankind." The pattern is 1-2, 1-2, 1-2, 1-2, 1-2.

By composing lines in a fixed rhythmic form Homer provided clues to help reciters remember the words. If a bard inadvertently substituted another word, and if it did not fit the pattern, the mistake would often be obvious. For example, let's say the line was changed to: "Inflaming brandy, pernicious to mankind…" The rhythm is broken, for "brandy" has added an out-of-place syllable. Now the line scans 1-2, 1-2, 1, 1-2, 1-2, 1-2.

The original example above, called a couplet, also demonstrates the second kind of memory cue Homer used, rhyming. Just as the pattern of syllables within the lines provided hints to future reciters, the rhyme helped them keep lines together. By requiring the rhyme, the first line cues the second. Today we call these internal clues mnemonics, things to assist the memory.

We seldom see the form of rhyming couplets today, but there is much that a modern writer of prose can learn from a study of Homer's craft (even though most of us see it only second hand through translation). He may have wanted to make his sagas easier to memorize, but there can be no question that his primary intention was to create words of power, giving his tales the ability to thrill listeners and rivet their attention.

Putting together words in ways that flow smoothly is a vital skill, for otherwise you can end up with something ugly, a jumble of awkward phrases that butt against one another in chaos and disorder.

Look at the difference a few changes can make. Here is the final line of Alfred Lord Tennyson's poem "Ulysses," written in the same iambic pentameter form as English translations of Homer (and referring to one of the Homeric heroes):

* * * * *

To strive, to seek, to find, and not to yield.

What if Tennyson had instead chosen to write:

To attempt, to look for, to come across,
     and not to capitulate.

Not quite the same, is it? The words are "right," but only as far as their definitions. Each substitution is a close synonym of the original words used by Tennyson, but the rhythm is atrocious and the meaning is clouded to say the least. What was a smooth, flowing line has become an ugly hash, a nasty knot of ill-fitted words.

What applies to poetry applies as well to prose, but without the need for strict patterns of rhythm or rhyme. (Much of what is today called poetry has more in common with prose.) In fiction the ways in which characters use words are important clues to their nature. No writer today would want a character to speak lines that may have come from Homer, Tennyson or Shakespeare. And yet, the rhythm of a written piece, the way in which words flow and meet and mingle, is an all-important element that distinguishes good writing from bad.

Sir Winston Churchill was said to have written his speeches in a kind of blank verse style, the better to flow from his tongue. He knew the importance of rhythm and flow.

The rhythm and flow of prose relates to the *sound* of the piece. That's different from *style*, which is embedded in sentence structure, and *tone*, which signals the intentions of the author (i.e., sarcastic, comic, intimate and so forth).

Another facet of writing is *pace*, the speed with which your story unfolds. You don't want your narrative to simply plod along at the same rate, for that violates the first rule of good writing: *Never be boring*. The words you choose and the way you structure sentences gives you the power to speed up or throttle back. Dialog is easy to read and so it usually serves to speed things up. We'll look at style, tone and dialog in later chapters.

When I was an aspiring writer in my early teens, both William Faulkner and Ernest Hemingway still lived and were among my boyhood heroes. I read every one of their novels and short stories. Their special ways with words awakened in me the recognition that mere words could be used to craft written pieces having special qualities of energy, a kind of magic that sets them beyond the ordinary. But oh! what a difference between the two.

Faulkner was known for his stream of consciousness style, where words were allowed to flow in rich profusion like thoughts passing through the minds of his characters. Run-on sentences, fragmented phrases – Faulkner broke every rule in the English Teacher's Handbook. And yet, there is rhythm and flow that make the words speak off of the page. Here is an excerpt, a single flowing sentence, from his 1948 novel *Intruder in the Dust*, describing the collective Southern memory of Pickett's Charge:

> For every Southern boy fourteen years old, not once but whenever he wants it, there is the instant when it's still not yet two o'clock on that July afternoon in 1863, the brigades are in position behind the rail fence, the guns are laid and ready in the woods and the furled flags are already loosened to break out and Pickett himself with his long oiled ringlets and his hat in one hand probably and his sword in the other looking up the hill waiting for Longstreet to give the word and it's all in the balance, it hasn't happened yet, it hasn't even begun yet, it not only

hasn't begun yet but there is still time for it not to begin against that position and those circumstances which made more men than Garnett and Kemper and Arm- stead and Wilcox look grave yet it's going to begin, we all know that, we have come too far with too much at stake and that moment doesn't need even a fourteen- year-old boy to think This time."

Hemingway wrote in a far different style. He was known for the pithy simplicity and brevity of his sentences. Where Faulkner reached for flowery and complex garlands of words, Hemingway chose the bare bones of short sentences constructed of simple words. He was Yin to Faulkner's Yang. He once advised: "Write poetry into prose."

Here is a passage from Hemingway's 1929 novel *A Farewell to Arms*:

If people bring so much courage to this world the world has to kill them to break them, so of course it kills them. The world breaks everyone and afterward many are strong in the broken places. But those that will not break it kills. It kills the very good and the very gentle and the very brave impartially. If you are none of those you can be sure it will kill you too but there will be no special hurry.

Two very different writers, two quite separate styles, and yet in both cases the words work, the phrases flow, the meaning is clear. They engage readers, making us think and feel.

Like all good writing, these examples ride on a wave of rhythm, a flow that carries us along from phrase to phrase, chapter to chapter. Writers such as these weave from words of power all that can be found in the human soul — emotions, ideas, sympathy, shame, pride, fear, hunger, desire, greed, kindness, good and evil –

all of those and many more. For that is the power of words well wrought.

But it isn't easy, for writing must seem natural to the eye and ear. Write with rhythm and flow that's too obvious, use too many "flowery" words, and you will be perceived as an amateur at the art of writing. The desired effect is to use the tools of rhythm and flow in subtle ways that carry the reader along on an inviting pathway of words.

There are other tools of the poet that can make your prose flow smoothly. Let me be clear that I don't want you to write poetry, but to apply the methods of the poet in small doses to bring your prose to vibrant life.

Assonance is a recognized poetic tool consisting of repetition of identical or similar vowel sounds. Here's an example, with some of the vowels highlighted, from Dylan Thomas's poem "Do Not Go Gentle Into That Good Night":

> Do not go gentle into that good night,
> Old age should burn and rave at close of day;
> Rage, rage, against the dying of the light.

Assonance can be used in prose as well as in poetry, but again be warned that the use must be subtle. Long vowels, especially the long O and long A, can create somber moods. Here is an example, from Cormac McCarthy's novel *Outer Dark*, describing the discovery by a mother of a site where her baby has been murdered:

> And stepping softly with her air of blooded ruin about the glade in a frail agony of grace she trailed her rags through dust and ashes, circling the dead fire, the charred billets and chalk bones, the little calcined ribcage.

The assonance of vowels, particularly long A's, helps make this scene come to life in all its horror. Note that McCarthy also makes use of poetic meter in some parts: "And stepping softly with her air of blooded ruin..." for example, clearly has a poem-like meter.

Just as assonance plays on the relationship between vowels, *alliteration* is the alignment of words beginning with the same consonant. Extreme examples include: "She sells sea-shells by the seashore," or "Peter Piper picked a peck of pickled peppers." Chances are you don't want to use such obvious alliterative combinations, but when applied with caution they can give a sentence a nice ring.

J. K. Rowling is known for her use of alliteration. Here's an example from one of the Harry Potter books, *Order of the Phoenix*:

> ...he had hidden himself behind a large
>   hydrangea bush...

The repetitive use of the letter "h" is subtle; it does not jump out at you and say "Boo!" like the "Peter Piper" type examples.

Here's another example of alliteration in prose, this one from James Joyce's *Portrait of the Artist as a Young Man*:

> Soft language issued from their spitless lips as they swished in low circles round and round the field, winding hither and thither through the weeds.

Here's another example, typically terse, from Hemingway's *The Old Man and the Sea*:

> I'll kill him though," he said. "In all his greatness
>   and his glory.

Again, note the accompanying use of poem-like meter in the

last phrase, 1-2, 1-2, 1-2, 1-2. The repetition of the word "his" makes the meter work, for without that addition the words "all his greatness and glory" would fall flat, lacking the power of Hemingway's rhythm. Here's an additional observation about this passage: Hemingway presents the second part of the statement in the form of a separate (and incomplete) sentence. The object, "him," is found in the preceding part. Real people seldom speak in complete sentences, and neither should fictional characters.

J.R.R. Tolkien pointed out that alliteration depends not strictly on letters, but on sounds. Thus, "know nothing" is alliterative. Incidentally, Tolkien used alliteration in many of his poems of Middle Earth, lines such as these from "The Muster of Rohan:"

> Farewell he bade to his free people,
> hearth and high-seat, and the hallowed places
> where long he had feasted ere the light faded.
> Forth rode the king, fear behind him,
> fate before him. Fealty kept he;
> oaths he had taken, all fulfilled them.

Tolkien modeled his poetry of Middle Earth after the Old English or Anglo-Saxon language of which he was a leading scholar. Alliteration was an important poetic tool in that linguistic ancestor of modern English, no doubt filling a similar role to Homer's meter and rhyme as memory enhancers.

Keep in mind that Tolkien used this heavy-handed alliteration to capture the flavor of the ancient time in which his fictional Middle Earth was set. You certainly cannot get away with using such obvious alliteration in everyday writing, but when used sparingly and with caution, it can be an effective tool.

Another poetic method that can be borrowed for prose is *consonance*. Just as assonance relies on repeated vowels, consonance uses repetition of consonants in close proximity. A related form is known as *sibilance*, the repeated use of "s" sounds, such as in this clever definition of the term: "the use of several sibilant sounds." Edgar Allan Poe was a master of the use of consonance and sibilance, easily apparent in his poem "The Raven," with lines such as this:

* * * * *

> And the silken sad uncertain rustling of each
>   purple curtain.

This is an example of sibilance, and note the demonstration of Tolkien's observation that it's the sound, not the letters, for the "c" in "uncertain" fits into the string of sibilant "s" sounds. This line also contains an example of assonance – the "ur" sound in the last two words.

I will end by mentioning yet another, if less important, word form, *onomatopoeia*, in which words for sounds imitate the sound itself. A few examples are "quack," "boom," "howl," "scratch," and "croak".

So why do we need to think about all these tricks of the poet's trade? I'll use metaphor to craft a reply. Fine cuisine requires large quantities of primary foodstuffs such as vegetables, meat and grain, but a master chef would be lost without the tiny amounts of spices, herbs and essences he uses to flavor his dishes. Those seasonings can make the difference between an ordinary and boring meal and a very special dining experience.

In the same way, by adding a few pinches of rhythm and flow, a dash of assonance, a touch of alliteration, perhaps just a hint of consonance and the occasional bang! of a pistol shot you can bring your stories to life. When applied with a light touch, these words of power can add sound and substance, scent and touch, flavor and zest, and yes, even excitement to your writing.

Chapter Four

Figuratively Speaking

What if I should tell you that most excellent writing is filled with statements that are not only untrue, but that refer to something completely different from the intended subject? And what if I added that those very things often help make the writing clearer to readers?

I am referring, of course, to the use of so-called figures of speech – *metaphor, simile* and other word tricks that compare one perhaps less familiar or complicated thing, idea, concept or image with another that is better known or easier to understand. Look closely at examples of superior writing and you will encounter these figures of speech everywhere. You may have noticed many examples in this book, for I am a firm believer in them.

Analogies are probably the most obvious and commonly used figures of speech, particularly metaphors and similes. Immanuel Kant saw analogy as "the wellspring of all creativity." Friedrich Nietzsche defined truth as "a mobile army of metaphors."

Metaphor is when the writer or speaker declares that a thing or concept *is* something else. The classic example is Shakespeare's line: "All the world's a stage."

Clearly the world is not a stage, but the metaphorical device helped Shakespeare express the image he wanted through comparison with something familiar to the audience, in this case the very stage on which an actor is speaking the line during a performance of *As You Like It*.

Simile is when the writer or speaker submits that one thing "resembles" another thing, through the use of a conjunction such as *like, as, so, than*. Similes are very much like metaphors, but allow room for doubt. For example: "My love is like a red, red rose" doesn't suggest that she actually is a rose. Neither does "He was as strong as an ox" imply a state of being an ox, nor "Her hand was as cold as ice" inform us that her hand would melt into water.

How can it be that by saying something other than what you actually mean, you can communicate your idea more clearly? In my opinion, it's because our curious brains constantly seek to find understanding by looking at parallels and comparisons to familiar things, as a way of understanding the world and the universe around us. I think in its simplest form this ability goes all the way down to the primitive brainstem we've inherited from reptilian ancestors of long ago. Here are a couple of examples of what I mean by that:

My late wife once had a little ceramic frog with its mouth wide open. One day she decided to put it outside under a flowering bush. I was sitting nearby when a hummingbird came to visit the bush. When it caught sight of the presumed hungry frog it let out a shrill cry of warning and zoomed away.

In a very basic way, the bird's brain had immediately associated the gaping mouth with danger. It's a metaphor: The big mouth *is* danger.

Another example: I notice that when I am walking in the woods and out of the corner of my eye see a stick lying on the ground, my mind immediately interrupts any other thought to ask: "Snake?" My brain processes the idea of something long and skinny as a potential danger. That's simile: the stick *is like* a snake.

On a very primitive level these are examples of *rhetorical analogy*, substituting one thing for another, in these examples in order to avoid potential danger. Thus, I suggest that responding to analogy is a natural function of any thinking creature.

Understanding how to use metaphor and simile is an essential step in becoming a superior writer. To make you more familiar with the power of these rhetorical tools, let's take a look at some examples. Here are a few well-crafted metaphors:

> Chaos is a friend of mine. – Bob Dylan, quoted in *Newsweek*.

> All our words are but crumbs that fall down from the feast of the mind. – Khalil Gibran, "Sand and Foam".

> A hospital bed is a parked taxi with the meter running. – Groucho Marx, as quoted in *Reader's Digest*.

> Let us be grateful to people who make us happy, they are the charming gardeners who make our souls blossom. – Marcel Proust, as translated from the French in *Les Plaisirs et les jours*.

> And your very flesh shall be a great poem. – Walt Whitman, from the preface, *Leaves of Grass*.

> Advertising is the rattling of a stick inside a swill bucket. – George Orwell, *Keep the Aspidistra Flying*.

In these examples of metaphor we see the direct statement that one thing is another, using the words *are, is, shall be* to denote the metaphorical statement of equality.

And here are some examples of similes:

> . . . she tried to get rid of the kitten which had scrambled

up her back and stuck like a burr just out of reach. – Louisa May Alcott, *Little Women*.

Her romantic mind was like the tiny boxes, one within the other, that come from the puzzling East . . . – J. M. Barrie, *Peter Pan*.

I would have given anything for the power to soothe her frail soul, tormenting itself in its invincible ignorance like a small bird beating about the cruel wires of a cage. – Joseph Conrad, *Lord Jim*.

In the eastern sky there was a yellow patch like a rug laid for the feet of the coming sun . . . – Stephen Crane, *The Red Badge of Courage*.

She entered with ungainly struggle like some huge awkward chicken, torn, squawking, out of its coop. – Sir Arthur Conan Doyle, *The Adventure of the Three Gables*.

He looks like right after the maul hits the steer and it no longer alive and don't yet know that it is dead. – William Faulkner, *As I Lay Dying*.

Her father had inherited that temper; and at times, like antelope fleeing before fire on the slope, his people fled from his red rages. – Zane Grey, *Riders of the Purple Sage*.

The very mystery of him excited her curiosity like a door that had neither lock nor key. – Margaret Mitchell, *Gone With the Wind*.

Camperdown, Copenhagen, Trafalgar – these names thunder in memory like the booming of great guns. – Charles Nordhoff and James Norman Hall, *Mutiny on the Bounty*.

He swung a great scimitar, before which Spaniards went down like wheat to the reaper's sickle. – Rafael Sabatini, *The Sea Hawk*.

...you've seen through me like a window that has no glass. – David L. Brown, *Sarah and the Dragon*.

Each of these examples uses the word *like* to introduce the simile, but do not forget that there are other options, including *as*, *so* and *than*.

Now it may seem that using analogies is a simple enough trick, but you should not be fooled. It's easy to wander into a swamp of confusion when metaphors and similes are poorly thought out. One of the most common mistakes is to create an analogy that doesn't really make sense or is downright silly. In July of 1995, *The Washington Post* announced a contest asking readers to submit examples of bad analogies. Here are a few of the finalists:

> I felt a nameless dread. Well, there probably is a long German name for it, like Geschpooklichkeit or something, but I don't speak German. Anyway, it's a dread that nobody knows the name for, like those little square plastic gizmos that close your bread bags. I don't know the name for those either.

> He was as tall as a six-foot-three-inch tree.

> The little boat gently drifted across the pond exactly the way a bowling ball wouldn't.

> Her eyes were like two brown circles with big black dots in the center.

> Her vocabulary was as bad as, like, whatever.

> John and Mary had never met. They were like two hummingbirds who had also never met.

> The red brick wall was the color of a brick-red Crayola™ crayon.

The sardines were packed as tight as the coach section of a 747.

The lamp just sat there, like an inanimate object.

And the top winner of the contest:

His fountain pen was so expensive it looked as if someone had grabbed the pope, turned him upside down and started writing with the tip of his big pointy hat.

These are amusing, but the point to be taken away is real. Analogies must have a kind of internal consistency, that is, the thing being proposed for comparison must provide a true parallel to the original and pass the common sense test. You cannot say: "The rock was like a soggy sponge," because rocks are hard and sponges are not, at least not soggy ones.

Another flawed example: "The Jeep's tires were like giant doughnuts." Since there is no such thing as giant doughnuts (as far as I know), the metaphor is meaningless. The object being compared to your subject must be logical and appropriate. In this example, the reader is given no useful point of reference.

Another common mistake is when a metaphor starts out to be one thing and then changes its mind halfway through, like a date who abandons you to dance with someone else at the senior prom. (Simile alert.)

For example, it just doesn't work when you write something such as "The landslide was like a runaway freight train that washed over the shore sweeping all before it," or "He pulled the trigger and the gun barked like a performing seal." These are just silly. Don't be silly.

Another problem arises when metaphors get mixed up. Here's an example from *The Chicago Tribune*:

So now what we are dealing with is the rubber meeting the road, and instead of biting the bullet on these issues, we just want to punt.

* * * * *

Now we can see a clue to how this mish-mash took place, for the statement uses several common phrases, *clichés*, which are individual metaphors. (This is a good reason to stay away from clichés, as we will see in a moment.)

There are other figures of speech that you can use to spice up your writing. For example, *hyperbole* is the use of exaggeration, in statements such as "The suitcase weighed a ton." This makes the point that the suitcase was heavy through exaggeration.

An *oxymoron* is a phrase such as "jumbo shrimp," "deafening silence" or "militant pacifist," where the point is to highlight the internal contradiction of the words, often for humorous effect.

There are a host of other figures of speech, too many to address them all here (by some estimates more than a hundred). Each can add a little touch of flavor to your writing, but like spices must be used with caution. Too much salt or pepper can ruin the dish. Here are a few more common figures of speech.

Clichés, as mentioned above, are trite phrases or expressions that have been over-used to the point that they have lost their power. You should avoid clichés like the plague. (Yes, I meant to do that.) Clichés make your writing look uninspired and ordinary.

It's not unusual to see and hear a certain cliché phrase being used again and again, things like "If all you have is a hammer, everything looks like a nail." If a certain figure of speech is in common usage, such as that one, don't use it.

However, that doesn't mean you can't take a once clever and fresh phrase that has become a cliché through overuse and turn it into something uniquely your own.

For example, here are some variations on the example above

that I jotted down one day when I'd seen the original cliché for about the thousandth time:

If all you have is a bun, everything looks like a hamburger.

If all you have is a screwdriver, everything looks screwy.

If all you have is a condom, everything looks like a penis.

If all you have is a Hellfire missile, everything looks like a terrorist.

If all you have is a Sousaphone, everything looks like a marching band.

If all you have is a shoehorn, everything looks like a shoe.

If all you have is a mousetrap, everything looks like a mouse.

If all you have is a broken paddle, everything looks like shit creek.

If all you have is a Navy carrier flotilla, everything looks like World War III.

If all you have is a turkey, it's a pretty poor excuse for Thanksgiving.

If all you have is a pair of socks, everything looks like feet.

If all you have is a ball bat, everything looks like a baseball.

If all you have is a lasso, everything looks like a cow.

If all you have is a fish hook, everything looks like Nemo.

If all you have is a spoon, everything looks like soup.

If all you have is a microscope, everything looks really big.

If all you have is a camera, everything looks photogenic.

...and finally

If all you have is a nail, watch out for hammers.

See how you can have some fun with words? Make your own clichés and you'll never have to say you're sorry. (Yes, on purpose.)

Idioms are common expressions that mean something different from their literal meaning, such as "raining cats and dogs" or "cost an arm and a leg." Many idioms have become clichés. Real people use idioms, and so should your characters.

Imagery is language that prompts sensory impressions, often visual but sometimes invoking sound, scent, touch or taste. Example: "The lake shivered under the touch of the morning wind." The reader is made to sense the effect of the wind by relating to the experience of shivering. Imagery is not actually a separate type of figure of speech, but can use metaphor, simile and other techniques to create feelings in the reader.

The poem "Daffodils" by William Wordsworth is filled with imagery, including metaphor ("a host") and simile ("...as the stars"):

> ...A host of golden daffodils;
> Beside the lake, beneath the trees,
> Fluttering and dancing in the breeze.
> Continuous as the stars that shine
> And twinkle on the Milky Way...

As with almost everything about writing, too much imagery will spoil the soup. It's one of those subtle spices that needs to be used with care.

Irony draws attention to the way things are expected to be and the way they actually are. Examples include the fact that the

Titanic was advertised as 100 percent unsinkable. Your characters can be made to seem more "real" if they observe and comment on the irony in events around them.

Paradox is a statement that seems to be contradictory but can express a deeper truth. For example, Oscar Wilde's line from "The Ballad of Reading Gaol": "All men destroy the things they love."

Puns are plays on words, substituting a similar word for the intended one, generally for humorous effect. Shakespeare was a master punster. Here, Romeo used a pun: "You have dancing shoes with nimble soles; I have a soul of lead."

Rhetorical questions are statements in the form of a question that is not intended to invite a response, but to make a point. A trite example: "Will this torment never end?"

There are many other lesser-used figures of speech. One thing that is common to all good writing is that a statement must have internal consistency and be logical. Here's a little anecdote from my past to provide an example of how muddled thinking can lead you astray. Back when I had my editorial services agency in Chicago, I once wrote a lead sentence for a feature article about a family farm in Virginia that started like this: "In the shadow of the Blue Ridge Mountains..." (Yeah, I know, cliché.)

Apparently inspired by my words, a few months later one of my staff writers submitted a story from Wyoming that began: "In the shadow of the Oregon Trail..."

Now, I've seen the Oregon Trail, and it doesn't cast much of a shadow. The writer apparently thought the "shadow" in my Virginia story was just some kind of clever analogy for something else, and that he could make my phrase into a cliché by applying it to his story. Didn't work. In fact, the shadow to which I referred was literal, something that took place every time the sun passed behind the mountains. Not true for the Oregon Trail. Out came my black editor's pencil.

* * * * *

Finally, to see how these literary devices are used in actual writing, following are a few examples by masters of the craft. Note that there is a notable lack of clichés and that the figures of speech are used with discretion.

So I learned to hold my tongue and turn my features into an indifferent mask so that no one could ever read my thoughts. – Suzanne Collins, *The Hunger Games.*

New sounds disturbed the moaning of the storm; the parched creak of a door, the mutter of a crumbling roof, the incessant sigh of wind upon a dying house. – John Le Carré, *A Murder of Quality.*

There was music from my neighbor's house through the summer nights. In his blue gardens men and girls came and went like moths among the whisperings and the champagne and the stars. – F. Scott Fitzgerald, *The Great Gatsby.*

Stories last longer than men, stones than stories, stars than stones. But even our stars' nights are numbered, and with them will pass this patterned tale to a long-deceased earth. – John Barth, *Chimera.*

It was the silent time between the thin birdsong of a March day and the hunting of the owls. – Mary Stewart, *The Crystal Cave.*

I had a farm in Africa, at the foot of the Ngong Hills ... The geographical position, and the height of the land combined to create a landscape that had not its like in all the world. There was no fat on it and no luxuriance anywhere; it was Africa distilled up through six thousand feet, like the strong and refined essence of a continent. – Isak Dineson, *Out of Africa.*

But, there were other echoes, from a distance, that rumbled menacingly in the corner all through this space

of time. And it was now, about little Lucie's sixth
birthday, that they began to have an awful sound, as of a
great storm in France with a dreadful sea rising. – Charles Dickens, *A Tale of Two Cities.*

Through practice and by studying the writing of masters such
as these, you can learn to weave your own passages into far more
interesting cloth; to catch up the imagination of your readers and
sweep them into your stories borne on waves of well-crafted words.
Words are exciting things, fun things. You can spend a lifetime
playing with them; you will find few more rewarding companions.

Chapter Five

Some Nuts and Bolts

Writing is a challenge because there are so many ways to express an emotion, action, scene or idea. It would not be unrealistic to say there are an infinite number of ways to tell a story. There are good ways, exciting ways, bad ways, boring ways, excellent ways and ways that are so absolutely dreadful they should never be seen by another pair of eyes. Let's look at some of the basic ways in which words are used to portray a story. This chapter will deal with the following areas in which the careful writer must make decisions:

> • **Point of view** (POV). Are you going to sit back and tell the story from an omniscient point of view; let the reader see the action unfold through the eyes of the protagonist or another character; or through some other method or combination of techniques?

> • **Voice**, whether active or passive. (Spoiler: active is almost but not always best.)

> • **Tense**. Will your story be told as something that happened "once upon a time," or like a movie unfolding moment to moment?

- **Format.** How do you break up and arrange the text for the best effect, such as with paragraph breaks?

POV can have a powerful effect on how the story is told. There are three basic positions from which the writer can weave his or her story: *first person, second person,* or *third person.* Now that sounds simple enough, but it can turn out to be more challenging than it seems.

First person is told from a character's point of view, and typically includes the pronoun "I" as the primary locator of the POV. This POV puts us inside the subject character. Example: "I watched Bob hit the ball."

First person narration brings the reader right into the action, perhaps even inside the character's head to see his or her thoughts and reactions. It can be very effective, especially when combined with active, present tense style. We'll see more on that later.

Second person is told as if the writer is addressing you, and is not often used in fiction. It is most appropriate for use in non-fiction books and articles, emails, business and technical writing, or presentations. Example: "You may if you wish end a sentence with a preposition." Second person places the narrator beside the subject character, like a mentor or guru. It's as if the writer is talking to you over a cup of coffee or a shot of Irish.

Third person POV is told from outside the subject characters. The traditional choice has been to write from the third person. In this form, the writer exists on a kind of separate plane above the action, looking down on the characters as they act out their roles. There are two main flavors of third person POV: *omniscient* and *limited.*

There are many advantages to the third person omniscient point of view, because it gives you the ability to move freely through scenes and among the cast of characters. In its omniscient form POV can switch at will, for example, from Frank who's trapped in a mine in Australia, to his wife Barbara fighting off an attacker in their home in New Jersey, to Judge Atkinson about to sentence Barney Stevens to prison for the murder of Sheriff Stone, to Barney's daughter lost in the North Woods while seeking evidence to prove her father's innocence – well, you get the idea. Writing in the omniscient third person is like being an all-knowing god.

Limited third person POV sees the action from a remove, but without the total freedom of an omniscient POV. In this form the action is viewed as if the writer is in a fixed location, often following the experience of the protagonist, and remaining unaware of outside events until we learn of them through the narrative.

Now here's where it gets interesting: You can switch from one POV to another within a story. For example, first we may see the action from the POV of Bob trapped in the mine, then to Barbara in New Jersey, then Judge Atkinson in his chambers and so forth. The writer "travels" from one POV to another as the story unfolds. This is known as third person objective POV.

And here's where it gets even more interesting: You can change between first and third person POV to keep your story moving. For example, during one scene you may be inside the protagonist's head as he tells the story as if he or she is the writer. In the next scene, you may switch to a sequence involving the antagonist and it could be told from a third person limited POV.

This is very much like the way motion pictures are structured, switching from one camera to another as the action unfolds. You may see the hero diving into the river to save the heroine from drowning, cut to a view of her clinging to a log, to a shot from the search-and-rescue helicopter overhead, and a clip of the cowardly villain making his escape.

Telling your story through more than one POV helps make it

more interesting, adding dimensions and depth that would other-wise be lacking. When you see things through the villain's eyes as well as that of the hero, heroine, or sidekick, helps you see the other characters in fresh ways. But here's a question: How many POVs are enough – and how many are too much?

The literary agent Albert Zuckerman in his book *Writing the Block Buster Novel*, answers those questions this way:

> I would recommend the smallest number possible, taking into account the story you are telling, but no fewer than three or four. With only one or two points of view, it becomes quite difficult to work up the kind of plot complexity and interpersonal drama readers expect in a big novel. With more than six or seven, the emotional focus tends to become diffused, and reader involvement with your lead characters is likely to diminish.

Zuckerman is writing about the kind of novel that presents a sweeping story, one of those 800-page doorstops that are so common these days, so the number of POV characters should be adjusted according to the scale of your work. In a short story, one POV might be appropriate, and a novelette might not support more than two. When writing a memoir, the POV should probably be the author alone, but remember that there are no rules.

Here are a few tips for working with POV:

> • Don't change POV within a scene. This can be extremely disorienting to the reader. A novel I was once asked to criticize started out with a character narrating in the first person POV – he was telling the story. About halfway through the chapter the author apparently realized that since the character was about to die, the first person POV was untenable, and without even a break changed abruptly

to third person as the character met his death. It was jarring, to say the least.

• When switching from one POV to another, it's probably a good idea to avoid having more than one character narrate in the first person. Like most rules this one is made to be broken, since it can be done effectively, so just be aware that readers may become confused if you're not careful.

• If you intend to change POV, it's best to do so at the beginning of a chapter or at a chapter break. Some believe no change should take place within a chapter, which may explain why some contemporary writers use very short chapters, in order to accommodate frequent changes of POV. (Another reason might be to fatten up a book to make it appear to be worth more by creating a lot of white space between tiny chapters. Yes, I can be cynical.)

• When changing POV, especially between first and third person, make sure it's clear which character's POV is in play. If there's a chance of confusion, identify the acting character right at the beginning of the new chapter or scene.

Don't unnecessarily filter facts through your characters. You don't have to write, "he saw the bird land on a branch," when it's enough to simply state "the bird landed on a branch." *He saw, she looked, he noticed* – these are filters that can take POV too far.

• When using third person POV and switching back and forth between characters, be sure to separate the changes. Here's a paragraph to demonstrate this point:

John swings and hits the ball just inside the third base line. Jerry sees it coming and picks it up on the bounce to tag out the runner coming from second. Whirling, he fires the ball across the diamond. Tom at first base snags the ball for a double play to win the championship.

This is slightly confusing since we jump from John's POV to Jerry's to Tom's, all within a single paragraph. An easy fix is to split the sentences with each man's POV into separate paragraphs. This is a subtle distinction. Note that making each sentence a separate paragraph adjusts the pace and makes the action palpable as each participant plays his part.

Voice comes in two flavors: *active* and *passive*. Active is almost always preferred. Continuing a baseball setting, here are two examples to demonstrate why this is true:

"The ball was hit by Bob."
"Bob hit the ball."

The first example is passive. The subject (the ball) is being acted upon. In the second example, the subject (Bob) is doing the acting. I don't need to say much about this, so I won't except for pointing out that the active voice is more concise as well as being direct and logical.

Tense is another area where the writer must make a decision. There are three basic forms: *Past, present* and *future*. As I've noted, most stories have traditionally been told in the past tense, as if relating some event from an earlier age. I've hinted that there are many good reasons to write fiction in the present tense (except perhaps when doing flashbacks). Here are my thoughts on this:

My last two novels, *Retirement Man* and *Sarah and the Dragon*, are written in the present tense, as if the action is taking place right now, not at some undefined time in the past.

Until recently, for the most part writing fiction in the present tense was considered a no-no. We're all familiar with the common past tense format of nearly every story or novel we've ever read. It's apparently *de rigueur* to take the position of a storyteller relating something that happened once-upon-a-time.

It's interesting that even science fiction stories set in the far future are usually written in the past tense. Well, of course, because that's just the way writing is done. It's one of those "rule" things.

But does it really make sense? Well, maybe not. After I started experimenting with the present tense in my murder mystery, *Retirement Man*, I soon learned to love telling a story that's happening in the here and now, just as the story unfolds. It puts the reader right into the middle of the action, and I like it. It gives the story a cinematic effect.

Now that I'm aware of it, I notice other writers who have used the present tense. For example, upon recently rereading William Faulkner's classic novel *Light in August*, I saw to my delight that it was in the present, not past tense.

Now many old-fashioned stick-in-the-mud writers and critics have a problem with this and they're quick to tell you why. It's unnatural, they say. It doesn't give the writer enough latitude, stuck in the present. It's just not the way writing is done. To all of which I call BS.

First, it's completely natural to speak in the present tense, so why not write in it? If you listen to a radio broadcast of a ballgame, does the announcer report the action in the past tense? It might sound like this: "Casey came to the plate. He swung at the ball but missed. Mudville was without joy."

No, that's not at all the way a sports announcer does it – it's present tense all the way. Casey steps to the plate, he swings the bat with a mighty stroke, etc. It's active, something that's taking place right now this very minute in the mind of the listener.

And by the way, if you look up the poem I'm alluding to, "Casey At the Bat," you may not be surprised to learn that it's written in...the present tense. To do it otherwise would ruin the whole effect, which raises the question: Why are most fiction pieces written in that plodding, boring, turn-the-readers-off past tense?

What about the claim that the present tense doesn't give the writer latitude? Who says writing in the past tense gives you more? It doesn't. When writing in the present tense I have the ability to do flashbacks and they go into the past tense, which is proper. I can move seamlessly between present and past tense as the situation requires.

If any form is limited, it's that old stodgy past tense. When you're already writing in the past tense, how can you differentiate a flashback from the main storyline? Unfortunately, there's no such thing as a past-past tense.* If you're writing in the past tense, you're stuck there and cannot go back any further.

I recently read a novel set in the present time but with numerous flashbacks to the Vietnam War. Strangely, the present time narration was in past tense, and the flashbacks were in present tense. In other words, just backwards from what common sense would dictate. I suppose the writer was trying to give the flashback scenes a different sense, which is a good idea, but for me the way he did it just didn't work.

---

* *In fact this is not precisely true, for there is a form called pluperfect that serves as a kind of past-past tense. However, it creates awkward phrases. Examples: "I had already eaten." or "He had written" instead of "he wrote."*

Another thing about writing in the present tense is that through its immediacy it creates a sense of tension – of "being there" – that keeps readers turning the page. To my mind, at least, it's harder to put down a story that's taking place right before your eyes (and unfolding inside your head in real time). The writer's challenge is to make the reader "experience" the setting, the nuances, the sights and smells and touch of the action. What better way than to tell it in the present tense?

Now there's another point I've read from critics, their claim that it's hard to write in the present tense. Does that mean one shouldn't do it? Of course not. It's a cop-out to claim otherwise. It's hard to become a concert pianist. It's hard to win Olympic gold. It's hard to do anything well, and that includes writing.

And frankly it isn't all that hard to learn to write in present tense, not at all. It took me a little while to master the full power and flexibility of writing in the present tense and after two novels it not only comes easily, but gives me a feeling I didn't have before, a sense of drawing the reader into my story as if he or she is sitting right beside me, under my spell as it were.

After I emailed the 80,000 word manuscript of *Retirement Man* to a friend, he wrote me the next day to say that he'd been up until midnight finishing the book, unable to stop turning the pages on his computer. That's the kind of effect you want to have on your readers, the ability to essentially pick them up and carry them along almost as if they themselves are characters in the story. Another friend who read the MS told me the characters seemed like "real people," not imaginary beings. That's the effect you want.

Some other comments I've read on the subject of present tense writing make the point that screenplay writers almost always write in the present tense, and indeed people who read my books often say they're reminded of a movie-like effect.

When written with skill, a book creates pictures in the minds of the reader, just as a movie flashes them on a screen. And not just images, for the written word can be far more powerful than any motion picture, which is limited to visual and audio effects. For example, words can express much more than just the sights and sounds of a car chase – it can bring to life the pulse-pounding reaction of the characters, the feel of cold sweat running down their necks, the smell of tire rubber, the spine-pounding thrust of the car seat, the thoughts and fears and hopes and doubts of the characters, and so much more. Can any movie do that?

So there's my position on writing stories in the present tense. I'm hooked on it. To me, it's become the natural, the correct way to tell a story. And as an aside I'd like to remind you that the passage of time itself comes in three flavors of which the most poignant, the most real, the most important is the present. The past is merely a collection of memories and the future is made of possibilities. Even though it is constantly moving, the present is where we're at, the place where we live.

The Roman poet Horace advised us to live for today. In the movie "Dead Poet's Society," the character played by Robin Williams put it this way: "Carpe Diem. Seize the day, boys. Make your lives extraordinary." If this is true, shouldn't our narratives take place in the all-important present?

Well, you can see that when it comes to this question of tense, I've become biased. I seem to have rewired my brain on this, because narration written in the past tense now seems somehow "wrong" to my eyes and ears.

If you don't buy my arguments in favor of present tense writing, or find it awkward or unsuited to your style, by all means continue to write in the past tense. You'll have lots of company, and there's nothing wrong with being part of the majority.

Meantime, here's that little example of active voice from above, edited to demonstrate past vs. present tense:

"Bob hit the ball."
"Bob hits the ball."

Somehow it seems to me that putting the active voice into present tense makes it even more – shall I say it – active? And the more action you can bring to your words the better.

Here's a final point: Past tense doesn't always relate to past time – it can also indicate a remote possibility that may come in the future. Example: "If you won the lottery, you wouldn't have to work." Another usage is when a verb is *backshifted*, i.e., to relate something that was said or took place in the past. Example: "I said that I was hungry," when in fact you would have said "I am hungry."

Finally, let's take a quick peek at format in writing. By that I mean how the words are arranged on the page. The primary objects of interest here are the sentence and the paragraph. Paragraphs are important because they not only keep the page from becoming a forbidding sea of gray, they allow you to pace your narrative, separate dialog between characters, assist the flow of ideas, or mark when there's a change in time or place.

There are many ways in which format can aid or hinder your readers. Linguists like to visualize sentences as trees, in which the words and phrases fit together like the trunk and branches and leaves. If this is so, then may we ask: What kind of tree do we want our sentences to be? Are they to be like stark shagbark hickories or a spreading sycamore? Should they hug the ground like a western juniper or soar to the sky like a giant sequoia?

The answer, of course, is that a good sentence can be any of those and more, from a leafless stalk to an entire fluttering grove of quaking aspens. Attempting to capture the living language in a net of rules is to chase the wind.

Paragraphs can be seen as little mini-stories in themselves. As such, they should say what they have to tell and no more. The flow of your narrative, discussed in an earlier chapter, can be adjusted through your choice of paragraph breaks.

Paragraphs can be short.

Or they can ramble on to express a complex scene.

In dialog in particular, they can be broken up into little pieces in order to create the effect you want, like this somewhat silly example:

> "Listen, you goon," Jack says, "I don't like..."
> "Lissen yerself," the thug interrupts.
> "...the way you're talking about..."
> "I'll talk how I want, jerk."
> "...my Mom."
> "Yeah, and I should care what you think?"

A good paragraph will serve you well by keeping the flow of your narrative and dialog moving at the pace you want. A bad paragraph can slow down or derail the momentum, and even confuse your reader, which is never a good thing.

Stephen King, in *On Writing*, says this:

> I would argue that the paragraph, not the sentence, is the basic unit of writing – the place where coherence begins and words stand a chance of becoming more than mere words. If the moment of quickening is to come, it comes at the level of the paragraph. It is a marvelous and flexible instrument that can be a single word long or run on for pages...

An excellent book is nothing but a series of excellent paragraphs. If you want to give your writing power, look at it paragraph by paragraph. Make each one count and you are well on the way to becoming a better writer.

There is another format tool, the chapter break. These are

when a scene ends and another begins. They are properly separated by an extra line spacing, like this:

Punctuation is an important tool in formatting your paragraphs and pages. Punctuation acts like traffic signs, indicating when the reader should slow down, stop, or make a turn to a new phrase or clause. They can help adjust the pace of your story, so it's generally a good idea not to use too much punctuation when you want the action to move ahead like the traffic on an interstate highway.

Your goal should be to bring your writing closer to spoken words, and that's where punctuation can help. Note that in the preceding sentence the comma is not strictly necessary, but helps the flow by serving the same function in writing as a brief pause in speaking. The result is to make the sentence clear to the reader.

Subordinate clauses, such as this one, should be set apart with commas to avoid confusion – and as demonstrated here, dashes can serve a similar role to help keep your thoughts flowing smoothly.

When words are skillfully punctuated, excellent writing may "sound" to the eye as if recited by an orator. But as always too much of a good thing can turn bad. Too many punctuation marks can yield a traffic jam when you want to keep the story flowing.

Italics and boldface are two other ways to help your reader stay on track by highlighting key words or phrases but this can easily be over-used. Remember that too much emphasis is none at all.

If your sentence contains a maze of phrases protected from each other by a squadron of commas, colons, semi-colons and dashes, chances are it's a failed sentence and can benefit from being quietly euthanized and replaced with something better. The writer Sir Arthur Quiller-Crouch once advised writers to avoid florid, overwritten prose by "murdering your darlings," but just plain awkward sentences need killing too.

Ask yourself: "Is that comma necessary?" If no, delete it. If the result is clumsy, see if you can edit the sentence to eliminate the need. Since punctuation slows down your reader, it's especially important to minimize it in passages with fast-paced action.

In general, aim for a Goldilocks balance – neither too much nor too little, but punctuation that's just right.

That's enough about these nuts and bolts of writing. There are far more nuances to the use of words than I've covered here, including different tenses that only an English teacher could love. Grammarians recognize 16 tenses and I have only addressed the simplest forms. If you want to learn more about that stuff, I suggest you find a book on English grammar.

If you've laid the foundations for becoming a good or excellent writer through extensive reading, the use of the language should come almost automatically. For now, let's get on to something more interesting: Characterization.

Chapter Six

Characters of Interest

Now that we've reviewed some of the tools you have at your disposal as a writer, let's start to see how you can apply them to bring times, places and events to life in the minds of your readers. It starts with those things called *characters*, the imaginary people that populate your fictional world.

(If you're writing a memoir, the same techniques can be applied to bring to life your real-world cast of characters. That's why I include memoirs in this discussion of fiction writing.)

Successful characters take on a kind of life of their own. After reading about them, who can forget such as Philip Marlow in *The Big Sleep*; Jeeves in *My Man Jeeves*; Stephen Maturin in *Master and Commander*; Jake Barnes in *The Sun Also Rises*; Holden Caulfield in *Catcher in the Rye*; or James Bond in *Casino Royale*?

The art of creating fictional beings is called *characterization*, and it comes in two flavors, *direct* and *indirect*.

The direct approach, as may seem obvious, is where the author describes the character. Here are a couple of examples:

> Her skin was a rich black that would have peeled like a plum if snagged, but then no one would have thought of getting close enough to Mrs. Flowers to ruffle her dress,

let alone snag her skin. She didn't encourage familiarity. She wore gloves too. – Maya Angelou, *I Know Why the Caged Bird Sings.*

He was most fifty, and he looked it. His hair was long and tangled and greasy, and hung down, and you could see his eyes shining through like he was behind vines. It was all black, no gray; so was his long, mixed-up whiskers. There warn't no color in his face, where his face showed; it was white; not like another man's white, but a white to make a body sick, a white to make a body's flesh crawl – a tree-toad white, a fish-belly white. As for his clothes – just rags, that was all. He had one ankle resting on t'other knee; the boot on that foot was busted, and two of his toes stuck through, and he worked them now and then. His hat was laying on the floor – an old black slouch with the top caved in, like a lid. – Mark Twain, *The Adventures of Huckleberry Finn.*

Indirect characterization is where you step back and let the character create himself through his thoughts, speech and deeds, or to be viewed through the eyes and thoughts of another character. Again, a couple of examples will serve to introduce this concept:

My brother Ben's face, thought Eugene, is like a piece of slightly yellow ivory; his high white head is knotted fiercely by his old man's scowl; his mouth is like a knife, his smile the flicker of light across a blade. His face is like a blade, and a knife, and a flicker of light: it is delicate and fierce, and scowls beautifully forever, and when he fastens his hard white fingers and his scowling eyes upon a thing he wants to fix, he sniffs with sharp and private concentration through his long, pointed nose...his hair shines like that of a young boy—it is crinkled and crisp as lettuce. – Thomas Wolfe, *Look Homeward Angel.*

For such an extraordinary athlete—even as a Lower Middler Phineas had been the best athlete in the school—he was not spectacularly built. He was my height—five feet eight and a half inches...He weighed a hundred and fifty pounds, a galling ten pounds more than I did, which flowed from his legs to torso around shoulders to arms and full strong neck in an uninterrupted, unemphatic unity of strength. – John Knowles, *A Separate Peace.*

Characters telling the story in the first person also can develop themselves, by recording their conscious thoughts, sometimes in stream of consciousness style. Here's an example, this from a personal memoir:

I didn't come to Utah to be the same boy I'd been before. I had my own dreams of transformation, Western dreams, dreams of freedom and dominion and taciturn self-sufficiency. The first thing I wanted to do was change my name. A girl named Toby had joined my class before I left Florida, and this had caused both of us scalding humiliation. ... I wanted to call myself Jack, after Jack London. I believed that having his name would charge me with some of the strength and competence inherent in my idea of him. The odds were good that I'd never have to share a classroom with a girl named Jack. And I liked the sound. Jack. Jack Wolff. – Tobias Wolff, *This Boy's Life.*

One of the most common failings I see in ordinary novels – those genres categorized as thrillers, action-adventure, fantasy, romance and so forth – is that the writers often emphasize action without bothering to create believable three-dimensional characters.

I believe a case could be made that this failing is what separates truly good fiction from the mundane. The imaginary actors in shallow stories are briefly described upon their first appearance, then left to march around through the unwinding plots like automatons, reacting to plot actions reflexively rather than from their own inner natures, of which little if anything has been revealed to the reader.

The same failing can be seen in many of today's motion pictures, often consisting of unending sequences of violent action created through computer graphics.

Since they have been created with only an outline sketch, such characters cannot express much if anything in the way of inner feelings, personal ideals, prejudices, special knowledge, fears, or any kind of human strengths or failings. They not resemble real people, but are more like puppets dancing on a tiny stage. They are mere cardboard cutouts, two-dimensional placeholders in the developing story.

All too often, to the extent they are described at all, the characters in such two-dimensional stories are physically and mentally remarkable – the women are always clever and beautiful beyond all compare; the men are tall and handsome, smarter than the average rocket scientist and likely trained in mystic martial arts. When given the opportunity, such couples invariably fall into bed and perform like actors in a porn video.

I'm reminded of the residents of Garrison Keillor's fictional Lake Wobegon, "where all the women are strong, all the men are good looking, and all the children are above average."

Such characters are, to put it nicely, difficult to believe. The writers might as well give them Super Powers and admit that their works are merely comic books drawn with words rather than pictures. Their output is what used to be called pulp fiction, and it has much in common with those B-level movies that go straight to DVD without ever appearing on a theatre screen.

Now I am sure that if we were to speak with an executive of a major publishing company, we would be assured these qualities of simplicity are absolutely demanded by their customers. And I am sure they have a point, for a certain kind of reader, but since you came here to learn how to write better than merely good, I suggest even the most outlandish plot actions can be carried out by three-dimensional characters. It's what makes the difference between a literary novel and those potboilers you read in a single sitting and throw away the next day feeling embarrassed for having read them.

It's through the effort of taking the trouble to create credible characters that make the reputations of some authors stand out over the years while the names of others sink into obscurity. Hemingway wrote thrillers. Faulkner wrote murder mysteries. But they wrote them in ways that engaged readers for many generations yet to come.

The novelist E. M. Forster in his book *Aspects of the Novel*, identifies characters as either *flat* or *round*, i.e., two-dimensional or fully formed. The nature of fictional characters can be further categorized as *dynamic* or *static*. Dynamic characters change and evolve during the course of the story, while static ones remain the same. The heroic main character is most likely dynamic and evolves. His butler, driver, bartender, barber and mechanic are likely static.

Don't bother to round out extraneous characters. For example, why bring up details of the garage attendant's life, how he's dressed and what's going through his head if all he's going to do is punch the heroine's parking ticket?

There are many fine writers producing thrillers, adventures, mysteries, fantasies and other categories of work. Their characters obtain stature through the hands of the author, assuming qualities that make them seem "almost real".

That's the goal you should set for your own characters. You want to create protagonists your readers can like, with whom they'd like to spend time, and villains that haunt their dreams.

If you set your sights on a higher goal, to write fiction of quality, perhaps even the Great American Novel, the ability to develop full-formed characters, ones that seem to step out of the pages almost as if real live people, is critical to your success.

How do you create a character? First, I believe you need to have a fair bit of experience in the real world, meeting and learning about real people. Only through such observation can you develop the ability to craft those imaginary people that come to life inside your head. It's a well-recognized truth that a writer must have a curious and observant mind, constantly packing away nuggets of information that might come in handy for some later purpose.

That doesn't mean that you should simply try to model fictional characters from actual individuals you've encountered. There is a reason why fiction usually carries a disclaimer that its characters bear no resemblance to any actual person, living or dead. But it *does* mean that you must draw upon real-life human characteristics to craft the actors in your stories.

By creating dynamic characters you'll make your story memorable. Characters should grow and evolve in tune with the developing plot, then act in ways that amaze and astound your reader.

Character development can be compared to a piece of music that starts with a simple tune played with one finger, then joined by the strings of a quartet and finally as your story reaches its climax swells to the power of a full orchestra. The secret is to start easily and build stage by stage. Don't try to force the full symphony down your readers' throats in the first chapter; keep the *Sturm und Drang* for the climax.

They say that curiosity killed the cat, and while that may be true an inquiring mind is a necessary part of becoming a master wordsmith. It's my experience that the characters I create are a kind of synthesis of many details from a wide range of people I've known, met in passing, or merely observed. Other character details have, of course, come from extensive reading that is every successful writer's foundation.

Just as words and phrases can include clichés, so can characters themselves be trite. If you create a character that is the living, spitting image of James Bond or Travis McGee, you have failed as a writer. Every living person is unique, with their own set of quirks and qualities that set them apart from others. So should your fictional characters be.

As a journalist and feature writer I've encountered many such exemplars, from judges on their high benches to crooks standing before them to receive judgment. In dealing with my late wife's many years of mental illness I've encountered doctors, psychiatrists, and mental patients alike. Son of a university professor, I grew up around a college campus filled with an eclectic array of scholars in many fields, and I was a curious campus brat who was always exploring and asking questions. I've traveled abroad more than the average person, always alert to the tastes, fashions, ideas, hopes and ideals of the people I meet.

Your background is different from mine, of course. We are like snowflakes, each similar in a broad general way while being wondrously unique. Each of us has our own special story to tell, and it's from that personal tale that you must draw the details of your fictional creations.

It's that special uniqueness that will give your stories power, adding hints of spice and seasoning to make them your own.

So how do we perform this magical act of creation that yields forth characters that seem almost to be real, performing actions to which readers can relate as if to events in the real world? It's not an easy task, and much of the art of characterization must come from experience, practice, and your inherent talent. Must we become like the woodcarver Geppetto who brought a wooden puppet to life in the story of Pinocchio? In a way, yes.

Here are a few ideas about the aspects of character creation to get you started in the right direction.

General guidelines. You must create in the minds of your readers an image of each character. This cannot be done simply by throwing in a paragraph when the character first appears, but must be an ongoing effort, continually adding little touches of insight about the character. What makes them think? How did they become what they are? Who nurtured their being? How do they judge others? All these and many more are questions that must be asked and answered, for they apply to the real people you wish to simulate through the power of words.

Physical appearance. It's necessary to allow the reader to create their own images of your characters, so it's a good idea not to go too far in describing them. Remember that we use our brains to think in metaphors and similes, and your reader is likely to focus his or her image of a fictional character on a real person from their own experience, such as an old friend or a film star. You may have John Wayne in mind, but your reader may see Tom Cruise. You need to give your readers enough physical detail to get them thinking in the right direction, but you don't need to show them the warts and all. (Except when the warts are important to your story. Remember: no rules.)

All your writer's tools can be used to draw the outlines of a character. Here is an example of an extended metaphor, variations on the theme of iron and the color gray (note the British spelling in the quotation), used to describe a village parson by Aldous Huxley in his 1921 novel *Crome Yellow*:

> In the midst of this brown gloom M.L. Bodiham sat at
> his desk. He was the man in the Iron Mask. A grey
> metallic face with iron cheek bones and a narrow iron

brow, iron folds, hard and unchanging, ran perpen-
dicular down his cheeks; his nose was the iron beak of
some thin, delicate bird of rapine. He had brown eyes,
set in sockets rimmed with iron; round them the skin
was dark, as though it had been charred. Dense, wiry
hair covered his skull; it had been black, it was turning
grey. His ears were very small and fine. His jaws, his
chin, his upper lip were dark, iron-dark, where he had
shaved. His voice, when he spoke, and especially when
he raised it in preaching, was harsh, like the grating of
iron hinges when a seldom-used door is opened.

The description gives no hint of approval for this dismal
character, telling us of a colorless and intolerant man.

I cannot pass this example without noting that I often see the
descriptive phrase "iron gray hair" and consider it a cliché to be
avoided. In this example, Huxley carries the analogy of iron and
grayness far beyond that common comparison. A character's hair
can be gray without allusion to the metallic substance. If you need
further description, use a fresh analogy, perhaps something like
"his hair was the dull, fading color of a rainy day," (but think up
your own phrase.)

Formative background. How did this character become what
he is today? What influences shaped her? What experiences have
they suffered? Where did they grow up? What education do they
have? All these can be introduced slowly. It doesn't pay to simply
hand the reader a *curriculum vitae* of the character upon first
appearance. That would be like piling a load of bricks in the
middle of your literary path. Introduce details as the story
proceeds, one bit at a time, as appropriate to the flow of the story.
Let your characters grow into their roles.

Often personal details can be revealed through conversation
between characters. Mastery of dialogue is a crucial part of effective
writing. (We'll visit this subject later.) Again, the picture should be

built up slowly and steadily as the story progresses. Strong, active characters never stop growing as they experience their fictional adventures or challenges.

Inner thought processes. What do the characters believe? How do they react to certain ideas? What are their internal codes of morality? Are they wolves or sheep? Do they act with confidence or are they burdened with doubt? Get your readers inside the heads of your creations and let them rummage around a bit. Again, slow and easy does it. Too much at one time will create reader overload. Establish these qualities then let them guide the characters' actions.

Provide rationale for your characters' actions. Sometime your story will require your protagonist to act in ways that would appear to be irrational. If you allow characters to go merrily along without providing the foundation for their otherwise inexplicable actions, they will come off as being naïve at best, stupid at worst. You don't want stupid characters in your story (unless you do), so give them a helping hand by explaining why they do what they do. And, of course, don't do it in an obvious way, but by providing clues and hints to the character's personal traits that allow your reader to understand their actions. In other words, weave the explanations into the whole cloth of the fully-formed character.

Don't make your characters into saints and sinners. Nobody's perfect and flaws make a character seem more real. Your reader needs to relate to your characters, even the bad guys. Give them human failings. Few villains are completely without compassion; no hero is perfectly assured. Let them have doubts, make mistakes, commit acts of kindness, cruelty or compassion. Real people are like that.

Show them to us through their possessions. The way your characters dress, the things they own and use, their jewelry, choice of weapon or car – all these are important keys to their nature. As a girl dresses up her Barbie to make it special, surround your characters with possessions and fashion choices that identify their nature and make them stand out.

Ian Fleming was well known for using this technique to frame the character of James Bond, listing by brand name Bond's choices of clothing, watch, car, gun, cigarette, liquor and many other items. In my opinion this can be overdone. Unless your purpose is to identify the hero's expensive taste, it's good enough to identify his watch as a stainless steel chronograph without mentioning the brand. In the ordinary course of events, injecting brand names can be a pointless diversion. And, of course, you must have a reason to refer to the watch in the first place.

Here's an example, from George Orwell's *1984*, in which the possession of a scarlet sash is used to provide insight into the character of Julia. Notice the use of irony, both in the choice of the color scarlet for an anti-sex symbol and how the sash actually emphasizes her feminine sex.

> She was a bold-looking girl of about twenty-seven, with thick dark hair, a freckled face, and swift, athletic movements. A narrow scarlet sash, emblem of the Junior Anti-Sex League, was wound several times around her waist of her overalls, just tightly enough to bring out the shapeliness of her hips.

Here's another example, the opening paragraph from Raymond Chandler's *The Big Sleep*. Hard-boiled detective Philip Marlowe describes himself, prepared to visit a potential client:

> It was about eleven o'clock in the morning, mid October with the sun not shining and a look of hard wet rain in the clearness of the foothills. I was wearing my powder-blue suit, with dark blue shirt, tie and display handkerchief, black brogues, black wool socks and dark blue clocks on them. I was neat, clean, shaved and sober,

and I didn't care who knew it. I was everything the well-dressed private detective ought to be. I was calling on four million dollars.

Show us how the character moves. The way she walks down the winding staircase; how he swings his legs out of bed; the way she chops carrots for a stew. Characters are not crash test dummies, but *faux* people and real people generally move in distinctive ways.

Here's an example from Susanne Collins's *The Hunger Games*. Notice how the author uses the character's birdlike posture to lead into an analogy that underlines the description.

> She's the twelve-year-old, the one who reminded me so of Prim in stature. Up close she looks about ten. She has bright, dark eyes and satiny brown skin and stands tilted up on her toes with arms slightly extended to her sides, as if ready to take wing at the slightest sound. It's impossible not to think of a bird.

Reveal them through their words. Dialog that is believable is a key to realistic fiction and we'll visit this subject in greater detail in a later chapter. The way your characters speak is vital to making them emerge as three-dimensional *persona*. I often see books in which every character speaks in complete sentences and follows the rules of grammar. Even characters lacking English as their primary language are often portrayed that way.

I strongly disagree. The way real people speak is an essential quality to their being, and if your fictional characters are to seem real, they must speak as real people do. That is to say, sometimes poorly, at least from the English teacher's point of view.

Is your character a Russian? Throw in a few common Russian words or phrases to remind the reader of that fact, such as having him assert "Nyet!" instead of "no," or mispronounce English words as a Russian might. Let him get his word order confused. Have him stop in mid-sentence, searching for an English word. Don't go too overboard with this. Keep in mind the spice and seasoning approach – a little goes a long way, but can make a big difference in how the reader perceives the character.

It's just as important to match language to characters that do speak English as their native tongue. There are many ways real people reveal their background and nature through their choice of words, grammar and vocabulary. Certain phrases or word choices can reveal insight into a character's nature.

An uneducated thug does not speak like an English teacher, and neither should your fictional thug. Your English teacher can speak like one if you wish her to, but almost no one else should (and even English teachers who are real people sometimes abuse the sacred rules of grammar and diction – they are, after all, human first and foremost).

And, here's a point that may surprise you: The rules I've suggested for you to follow, such as (cue voice of God): "Avoid Clichés Like the Plague," does not apply to your characters. They can use clichés as much as they want if it's in their nature to do so, because they are not you and are not bound by your self-imposed stylistic boundaries.

Superior writers avoid clichés when writing prose, but real people use them all the time, and so should your characters when it's appropriate. By writing dialog that puts banal words in a character's mouth you tell the reader something about the character. More imaginative characters should be allowed to exhibit their superior perception, throwing out an original wise-crack, witticism or pun from time to time to provide hints to their clever nature.

Here's an important lesson to draw from the above: Do not confuse your characters with yourself – they are different (if imaginary) people with their own faults, foibles and failings. As G. K. Chesterton wrote: "A good novel tells us the truth about its hero – but a bad novel tells us the truth about its author."

Do not let yourself become caught up in your characters – keep them separate and apart and let them be themselves. You may be surprised at how they seem to come to life on the pages, if you give them the freedom to do so. (I'm speaking of conscious association here; as I mentioned earlier in this book, I think our fictional characters come to life in large part through our unconscious minds, and in that way they might be seen as different aspects of ourselves.)

Here's another dogmatic rule to put in your writer's kit: Don't be afraid to let your characters speak in incomplete sentences. It isn't natural to consistently do so in ordinary speech. Listen to them speak by reading your work aloud. Do they sound like real people, or cardboard cutouts? Make them walk the walk and talk the talk. (And yes, that's a cliché, but appropriate in this case. Never forget that it's always okay to break rules as long as you do in consciously, and not too often.)

What about the use of obscenity? Many writers today invoke the "seven dirty words," often to excess. I personally prefer not to use this kind of language too much and try to avoid the f-word in most cases, although when appropriate to the way a character would speak, it's unavoidable. I know that rough language offends some potential readers, and we can't afford to lose them.

Use your judgment on this, and in particular with an eye to your target readership. Obviously, in children's and at least some YA stories it's forbidden to use the Not-So-Magnificent Seven. And for goodness sake, make sure the language fits your character.

Invoke the senses. No real person is made up only of a physical body, and neither should fictional characters be. Introduce qualities of your character's nature to all five senses in the reader's mind. Remember that it's okay to give your characters short-comings, for that will give them a sense of reality.

- Does he speak with a deep, almost thundering voice when angry?
- Does she sometimes lisp or stutter?
- Does her hair smell like fresh fallen rain?
- Does his hand bear the calluses of hard labor?
- Does her tongue taste of wildflowers when he kisses her for the first time?
- Do his tired joints creak when he stands up?
- Does he grunt with effort as he swings the axe?
- Does the priest murmur quietly in Latin as he dips his finger in the fount?
- Does the smoke make her eyes smart?

All these are examples that apply to qualities of your characters other than mere sight – invoking hearing, scent, taste and touch. Just as you should use all five senses to describe a scene or action, assign them the task of helping to round out your characters. We do not perceive a real person through our eyes alone, nor should we expect our readers to judge our characters in that way. Just as we perceive the world around us using all of our senses (and perhaps a sixth we might call intuition), so should we make it possible for our readers to enter and experience our imaginary worlds of words.

Another way to look at characterization is to consider the many English terms for specific individual qualities. These character traits include both positive labels (*honest, loyal, devoted, sincere, ambitious, patient, determined* and so forth) and negative ones (*unkind, rude, greedy, cruel, wicked, grumpy, selfish, conceited*). You can find extensive lists of these traits on-line or in a thesaurus.

Now I don't suggest that you merely pluck these words out of the air and hang them around the necks of your characters like the signs on a police mug shot. To write "He was honest, loyal and determined, although sometimes greedy and grumpy," for example would be a pretty dismal failure at creating a character. It would be clumsy and amateurish, consisting only of a series of sterile labels.

Instead, through the character's words and actions, and the reactions of others, demonstrate those traits you want readers to discover in the character. Creating a short list of traits for each member of your cast of characters can help you find ways to make them look real, but keep that list aside merely for your own reference.

Finally, and perhaps most important of all, show rather than tell your reader what you want them to know about your characters. Don't just say: "he was strong" (or certainly not "he was strong as an ox), but rather have him demonstrate the quality by picking up a heavy object or easily knocking aside an attacker. Don't just say: "she was smart" (and certainly not "she was smart as a whip"), but have her say and do things a smart person would.

By crafting your words to evoke pictures in your readers' minds, by showing them what you mean rather than telling, your characters will come to life on the page.

Another important aspect of characterization is to place each character in his or her proper role in the story. This is like a stage director marking out places for each actor on the boards. There are a number of basic character types, and just as a play calls for an interacting mix of characters, so should your story include a variety of different character types. Here is a brief look at some major categories.

The Protagonist. These are the main characters (in some stories there are more than one), the stars of the show, the ones through or about whom your story is being told. Sometimes the title of a book is the protagonist's name (Tom Jones, Oliver Twist,

Jane Eyre, Anna Karenina, Silas Marner). Sometimes the protagonist is not who you think. For example, Tolkien once said the main protagonist in *Lord of the Rings* was not Frodo as we might assume, but his faithful companion Samwise Gamgee.

The Antagonist. Every hero needs an anti-hero. The antagonist is the villain of the story, or at least a character that stands in opposition to the protagonist. Many famous characters from literature came from this important role. These include Jadis ("The White Witch") from C.S. Lewis's *Chronicles of Narnia*; Professor Moriarty from Sir Arthur Conan Doyle's *Sherlock Holmes* stories; Sir Leigh Teabing ("The Teacher)" from Dan Brown's *The Da Vinci Code*; and last but not least, Iago from Shakespeare's *Othello*. Robert Lewis Stevenson created an all-in-one protagonist-antagonist in his *Dr. Jekyll and Mr. Hyde*.

Other character types include the underdog, the sidekick, the mentor, the confidant, the foil, and so forth. In my experience, characters tend to find their own places in the story, but it may help you to assign them a category. Don't be surprised, however, if ones you brought on as stock characters begin to exhibit unexpected qualities, and even rise to become major characters as the story unfolds.

This is especially true for those of us who are "cats," letting the stories spin themselves from our unconscious minds. For example, in my novel *Sarah and the Dragon*, a character introduced as an Islamic terrorist and assassin (an antagonist) evolves and becomes a companion to the heroine (a protagonist). One lesson from this is that fully-rounded fictional characters, like real human beings, can and must change.

Here's one final aspect of characterization: How to pick appropriate names for your characters. There are a few definite rules to follow: Do not name your characters after famous people, particularly living ones. Sure, George W. Bush has a nice ring to it, but it's not a very good choice for a character that is not the former president. Similarly, the names of characters from other authors should be avoided, unless you want to create an ironic effect. Yes, there is a singer named Tom Jones and a magician named David Copperfield, but this is dangerous ground. You must certainly not use names that are even slightly similar to current established literary characters, such as Jason Bourne or Jack Reacher, for that is a sure path to a courtroom.

Pick names that are relatively easy to pronounce, since the reader will want to run them around on his or her tongue. Should your book be issued in an audio or speech-enabled e-book edition, your attention to this will be much appreciated.

Many literary names do not include a middle name, especially for evil characters such as murderers. This helps avoid lawsuits from real people who have the exact same names. It's also not a good idea to name your hero something like James Earl Ray or Jeffrey Dahmer.

Ian Fleming once described how he chose the name James Bond for his signature character:

> I wanted the simplest, dullest, plainest-sounding name I could find, 'James Bond' was much better than something more interesting, like 'Peregrine Carruthers.' Exotic things would happen to and around him, but he would be a neutral figure—an anonymous, blunt instrument wielded by a government department.

A friend of mine once asked me to look over a draft of his novel, and I discovered that he had adopted by name an entire cast of characters and even background and settings from a popular television show. I told him I was sure the producers would have a problem with that, and he shrugged it off, saying: "I'm sure they won't mind." He had no idea of the power and ruthlessness of the

American legal system and the lengths to which corporations such as Disney and MGM are prepared to go to protect their intellectual property.

Using alliteration of initial letters makes a name stand out (Severus Snape, Bilbo Baggins, King Kong). Readers sometimes have trouble keeping your cast of characters straight in their minds, especially if there are a lot of them, so cues such as this can help them identify who is "on stage" at the moment in your plot.

Consider the underlying meaning of a name. For example, don't give characters names that conflict with the qualities with which you endow them. Examples: Cecelia means "blind"; Deidre means "sorrowful;" Portia means "pig;" Byron means "cow barn;" Calvin means "bald;" Campbell means "crooked mouth."

Make the names appropriate to the times and places in which your story is set. It would not make sense to name a native Parisian Sven or Ivan. Susie Wong is a good name for a Eurasian woman in Hong Kong, but would be a lot less believable if she lives in Butte, Montana and is a full-blooded Sioux. If your story takes place in Ancient Rome, names like Billy Bob or Ginny Sue might not ring true.

Vary the first letters of your characters names. Giving several characters names starting with the same letter may create confusion.

The way I come up with character names is to go through a telephone book and write down names that catch my eye. I do not take full names, just first or last, making separate lists. Then I pick from each list like ordering from a Chinese menu to create a name for each character as he or she enters the stage, scattering them around across the alphabet.

Another consideration is how many characters to have. Some critics say the list should be short. The story of the Garden of Eden has just four characters; *War and Peace* has scores of them.

Neither is right or wrong. It depends upon your story – you need exactly as many characters as it takes to tell it well. If you're writing of a single man's struggle against nature, as Hemingway did in *The Old Man and the Sea*, one character is enough. If you're telling a complex story of conflict between feuding factions, you probably need to populate your book with a full cast. There is no rule other than that of common sense. Every character must have a purpose.

One final word about characterization: Use words of power to describe your characters, calling on all the tools of a writer to create images in the minds of your readers. Here are a few introductory descriptions of characters from well-known works.

> The face of Elrond was ageless, neither old nor young, though in it was written the memory of many things both glad and sorrowful. His hair was dark as the shadows of twilight, and upon it was set a circlet of silver; his eyes were grey as a clear evening, and in them was a light like the light of stars. – J. R. R. Tolkien, *The Fellowship of the Ring*.

> Mrs. Dursley was thin and blonde and had nearly twice the usual amount of neck, which came in very useful as she spent so much of her time craning over garden fences, spying on the neighbors. – J. K. Rowling, *Harry Potter and the Sorcerer's Stone*.

> We wore our best dresses on the outside to make a good impression. Rachel wore her green linen Easter suit she was so vain of, and her long whitish hair pulled off her forehead with a wide pink elastic hairband.... Sitting next to me on the plane, she kept batting her white-rabbit eyelashes and adjusting her bright pink hairband, trying to get me to notice she had secretly painted her fingernails bubble-gum pink to match. – Barbara Kingsolver, *The Poisonwood Bible*.

> A heroic belch of thunder followed the strange little man into the shop. He glanced around apologetically, as if the

rude noise were his responsibility rather than nature's, and fumbled a package under his arm so he could close a black-and-white-striped umbrella. ... Both umbrella and man dripped, somewhat mournfully, onto the neat square of mat just inside the door... He stood where he was, as if not entirely sure of his welcome. – Nora Roberts, *Hot Rocks*.

His wiry gray and black hair was dripping with sweat, and his face was the color and texture of old paper. He looked up at me from where he was seated on his bunk, and his eyes were hot and bright and moisture was beaded across his upper lip. He held a Camel cigarette between his yellowed fingers, and the floor around his feet was covered with cigarette butts. – James Lee Burke, *The Neon Rain*.

Now that you've gotten a feel for how to populate your work with casts of three-dimensional characters, let's proceed to the next step: Creating believable settings for your story, memoir or novel.

Word Power

Chapter Seven

Putting Characters in Place

Once you've created a cast of characters for your story, it's of almost equal importance to create effective settings in which to place the action. The places where your fictional children will work, play, love, live and sometimes die are of vital importance to the success of the whole.

No story can exist in a void. Harry Potter must have his Hogwarts, Frodo his Middle Earth, and Superman his Metropolis. Just so, your story must have settings that provide a proper sense of reality as your story unfolds.

The novelist Eudora Welty once said:

> Every story would be another story, and unrecognizable if it took up its characters and plot and happened somewhere else... Fiction depends for its life on place. Place is the crossroads of circumstances, the proving ground of, What happened? Who's here? Who's coming?...

In general there are two kinds of settings: the real and the imaginary. Hogwarts, Middle Earth and Metropolis are imaginary, but many stories are told in places that exist in the real world, such as Paris, New York City, ancient Rome or the frozen wastes of Antarctica.

There is a third dimension to this subject, and that is time. Is your setting in today's world, the historical past, or some unknown future? Most science fiction stories are set in the future. Thrillers, mysteries and such tend to be set in today's world, and many romances and all historical novels in familiar past times. Fantasy stories often take place in some otherworld beyond our ken, disconnected from our sense of time.

Real settings may seem easiest, because the places actually exist and it's up to the writer merely to accurately portray them. It's actually quite hard, because as always the words must be more than good.

To describe any real place in a way that approximates the reality is a significant challenge, because the reader may be intimately familiar with the setting and may be quick to see the glitches and flaws of a heavy-handed treatment. It could be argued that it's easier to write imaginary settings because no one can find fault with your description, at least on a factual basis.

Let's compromise on the question of which is harder and agree that all settings are difficult to create effectively, whether downtown Chicago or alien Star-City on Vega VII.

Similarly, historical settings are tricky because they are widely known. To capture a believable picture of past settings you must do your homework and learn the details of the time. It won't do to have historical characters appear in inappropriate places, or to inadvertently introduce anachronisms, things that are out of place in time. Some examples of anachronisms would be to have a Revolutionary War soldier using a revolver; a Roman Senator checking his wristwatch; or even a character in the 1970s using a cell phone.

When you set out to write about a real setting, you need to

know something about the place, either through personal experience or research. If you're serious about your project, by all means visit the settings – walk the streets and alleys, sample the food, listen to the sounds of the crowds, smell the sweet blossoms, observe the way the wind blows and the clouds come up over the mountains in mid-afternoon.

If you cannot do research on-the-ground, the next best thing is to read about the place you intend to use as a fictional setting. Travel guides are a good place to start. There's a world of information available on the Internet about almost everyplace in the world. Local histories, memoirs and essays are other good sources of facts about times and places.

Imaginary settings face you with a different set of challenges. Your readers have no knowledge of the stage on which your characters will act and speak their lines. It's up to you to make the imaginary place seem real. Your reader will not know its history, so you must provide it. There may be strange plants and animals not found on this earth, and you must describe them and do it in such a way that your reader can visualize what exists only in your imagination.

Again, masterful use of words is the key to making a setting work for your story. Some authors go to great lengths to create their fictional worlds. Tolkien wrote a history for Middle Earth in his book *The Silmarillion*. Frank Herbert wrote extensive background for his novel *Dune* and a number of sequel and prequel novels, some written after his death by his son and a co-writer based on Herbert's detailed notes.

Imaginary settings can take place in our time and with reference to real places. For example William Faulkner set many of his Southern novels in non-existent Jefferson, Mississippi; in his eponymous novel, Sherwood Anderson wrote a series of stories set in fictional Winesburg, Ohio; Harper Lee's *To Kill a Mockingbird* is set in Maycomb County, an imaginary region of southern Alabama.

When imaginary settings are introduced in the real world, it gives the writer a double challenge, but it makes for interesting effects. For example, Harry Potter and his friends travel aboard the magical Hogwarts Express from Kings Cross Station in more-or-less the real London of today to an entirely imaginary Hogsmeade Station.

Settings can be used to establish atmosphere or mood, serve merely as a backdrop for action, act as a metaphor for the theme of the story, or actively affect the characters. Perhaps surprisingly, the setting can actually serve as a kind of character.

Think of *The Old Man and the Sea*, in which the powerful Gulf Stream serves as antagonist to the old fisherman. Yes, things can act as characters. If a story concerns a man's efforts to climb a forbidding mountain, in a way the mountain itself becomes the antagonist.

The choice of setting for your action scenes can make a big difference. By letting events take place in a different, more interesting place, you can often add to the dramatic effect. Sometimes an exotic setting is appropriate, but in others you may want to downplay the sense of place, letting the action stand out from a neutral background.

Below is an example of how a setting can establish mood, from Edgar Allan Poe's story "The Fall of the House of Usher." Note how Poe weaves action and setting to move his story forward.

> During the whole of a dull, dark and soundless day in the autumn of the year, when the clouds hung oppressively low in the heavens, I had been passing alone, on horseback, through a singularly dreary tract of country; and at length found myself, as the shades of the evening drew on, within view of the melancholy House of Usher.

In a similar way, Emily Bronte always created a depressive mood when describing the house for which her famous book is named. In chapter 12, for example, she writes:

> There was no moon, and everything beneath lay in misty darkness; not a light gleamed from any house, far or near all had been extinguished long ago; and those at Wuthering Heights were never visible...

In the following example from his short story "A Rose for Emily," William Faulkner establishes the setting while telling us something about Miss Emily's resistance to change:

> It was a big, squarish frame house that had once been white, decorated with cupolas and spires and scrolled balconies in the heavily lightsome style of the seventies, set on what had once been our most select street. But garages and cotton gins had encroached and obliterated even the august names of that neighborhood; only Miss Emily's house was left, lifting its stubborn and coquettish decay above the cotton wagons and the gasoline pumps – an eyesore among eyesores.

Here's another example, from J.K. Rowling's *Harry Potter and the Order of the Phoenix*, showing how setting can help establish mood:

> The walls were made of dark stone, dimly lit by torches. Empty benches rose on either side of him, but ahead, in the highest benches of all, were many shadowy figures. They had been talking in low voices, but as the heavy door swung closed behind Harry an ominous silence fell.

In my own novel *Quantum Cowboy*, the main setting is the Los Alamos National Laboratory, and yet as I note in the endnotes, the details are completely imaginary. This is an example of a real setting that is twisted for the purpose of the story.

Settings that affect characters are common in literature. For example, a protagonist who grew up on the mean streets of Harlem will exhibit quite different qualities from one born to a ranch in Montana or a small town in Alabama. What would Scarlett O'Hara be without Tara, her fictional plantation in *Gone with the Wind*? Could Big Brother have become a powerful antagonist without the future setting of Oceania in *1984*? Could the character of Jay Gatsby have flourished anywhere but in the Hamptons?

So-called local color provided by an exotic setting can provide a touch of spice to your story, but should be used with caution. It's easy to focus on the quirks and peculiarities of a setting to the detriment of your story. Make sure any local color actually contributes to character development, conflict or action, rather than becoming a distraction.

Here's how Harper Lee introduces the fictional Southern town that is the setting for *To Kill a Mockingbird*:

> A day was twenty-four hours long but seemed longer. There was no hurry, for there was nowhere to go, nothing to buy and no money to buy it with, nothing to see outside the boundaries of Maycomb County.

As we can see in this example, settings don't have to be defined only by their physical features. Here, Lee gives us a feeling for the psychology of the place, a region dominated by hopelessness, disconnected from the outer world. In this cheerless setting she places Tom Robinson and Atticus Finch to act out their story.

Just as you should not attempt to cram a whole character into a paragraph or two, settings should be built up slowly while keeping the story moving. Don't over-describe a setting. The novelist Roger Zelazny proposed a "rule of three," limiting descriptions to no more than three items at one time. Add features in stages as appropriate, for example when a character enters a particular place.

It's good advice to leave out details that aren't necessary to the action, a principle stated by novelist Anton Chekhov. In his rule called "Chekhov's Gun," he advised:

> Remove everything that has no relevance to the story. If you say in the first chapter that there is a rifle hanging on the wall, in the second or third chapter it absolutely must go off. If it's not going to be fired, it shouldn't be hanging there.

This has come to be known as *foreshadowing*, the introduction of details in the setting or actions of characters that set up or predict a future action. I would not take Chekhov's advice too literally, since the description of details in a setting can reveal facts about a character without having to resort to openly stating it. Real people surround themselves with personal items that are clues to their natures or pasts, and so should fictional characters. In that way a mentioned item can serve its purpose without having to be employed in later action.

Sometimes another device, called a *red herring*, is introduced in order to mislead the reader, as for example to lead them to suspect the butler did it when all along it was the gamekeeper's daughter.

Here's another point to keep in mind: It's a good idea to avoid using coincidental events to get out of plot difficulties. Yes, coincidences do take place so you are allowed one relatively minor one in each story, but to use more will stretch credibility.

Ancient Greek plays often ended with seemingly insoluble conditions being resolved through what came to be known as a *deus ex machina*, an actor portraying a god lowered on a rope or rising from the stage. It's good advice never to use coincidence to resolve a major conflict or action, and to eschew the propitious arrival of helpful gods.

Finally, let's touch on another literary device called the *MacGuffin*, something that is introduced with no eventual point. Films often contain these little mind tricks, a method popularized by director and producer Alfred Hitchcock. In a 1939 lecture at Columbia University, he explained the term as follows:

> It might be a Scottish name, taken from a story about two men on a train. One man says, "What's that package up there in the baggage rack?" And the other answers, "Oh, that's a MacGuffin". The first one asks, "What's a MacGuffin?" "Well," the other man says, "it's an apparatus for trapping lions in the Scottish Highlands." The first man says, "But there are no lions in the Scottish Highlands," and the other one answers, "Well then, that's no MacGuffin!" So you see that a Mac-Guffin is actually nothing at all.

Examples of MacGuffins are the falcon statue in *The Maltese Falcon*; the meaning of "Rosebud" in *Citizen Kane*; the briefcases in *Pulp Fiction*; and the necklace "Heart of the Ocean" in *Titanic*. The last three examples are from motion pictures, but the concept applies to fiction as well.

That's enough on the subject of settings. Let's move on to an examination of how to design the framework of your story.

David L. Brown

Chapter Eight

Structuring Your Story

Much has been written about how stories ought to be told. Some claim there is a series of steps that must be followed to carry a story forward to completion. There have been entire books devoted to this subject alone. You may encounter such concepts as *inciting events, key events, plot points,* and *climax.*

My purpose in this book is to demonstrate how to use words of power, so I will touch lightly on this subject of structure. Clearly, most stories must be internally consistent and flow smoothly – in other words, have an invisible structure that holds them together just as an architect's plan describes the way a carpenter will construct a house. This is known as the *plot.*

There were no novelists in ancient Greece, but playwrights filled a similar role. No less a person than Aristotle decreed that all stories must be told in three acts. He defined them as *rising action,* climax or *crisis,* and *falling action.* This applied in particular to the tragic form, in which the protagonist is introduced in glory in act one, runs into trouble due to some personal fault (most often pride or hubris) in act two, and falls to a bad ending in the third act.

Some critics still argue in favor of the three-act formula on the grounds that every human action has three stages: before the action, during the action and after the action. Others favor four or five "acts" and some successful novels have so many ups and downs that it's hard to tell how many acts they contain. Scholars have tried to calculate just where in the storyline each stage should take place. These are rules, and as we've seen, rules are to be taken as foundational knowledge, not strict and unbreakable law.

All of this formula seeking seems a bit mechanistic to me, but I don't pretend to be an expert on the scholarly analysis of writing. In my opinion a story must:

- Introduce and develop interesting characters
    and settings;
- Create conflicts that bring crisis and demand resolution;
- Portray dramatic sequences of actions that
    keep the reader involved;
- Bring the story to a series of peaks that lead to a
    defining final crisis; and
- Do so in a way that is logical, internally
    consistent and satisfying.

This is by no means a complete model on which to structure your story, but any piece of fiction that fails to meet these minimal requirements is likely to fall flat. But, and this is an important caveat, short stories, memoirs and novels do not succeed or fail depending upon the order in which the story is told. If the author fails to put together words in such a way to intrigue the reader and maintain his or her interest through to the end, the entire edifice falls down. It's those powerful words that make the difference, in the way authors weave them together to keep the reader turning the pages right through to the final scene.

To return to the analogy of an architect's rendering, imagine how that metaphorical house would turn out if built by a completely incompetent carpenter? Not so well, I imagine. And in that same way, it doesn't really matter how much structure you bring to your story if the words are not crafted with skill and effect.

I'm not suggesting that you should ignore these ideas about the structure of your work. There is significant value to the idea of breaking down your story into steps. In general, it's usually necessary to establish the characters and settings early on; to build toward the peak action as the story unfolds; and to tie everything up in a neat package at the end. These must be done in the proper order, and without taking the reader off on wrong turns into irrelevant, boring, or confusing scenes.

As a rule-of-thumb you should probably introduce all major characters and themes in the first third of your story; devote the middle third to development; and the final third in resolving conflicts and bringing the story to a pleasing end. Like all rules, this one is made to be stretched if not broken.

To my mind, too many writers today – particularly those specializing in thriller, adventure and mystery novels – tend to lump everything all together in one long string of crisis and action. This is a structure that goes right for the throat. I recall that one well-established writer started a recent novel with the words "Bullets were flying past (name of character's) head". Some critics advocate starting the action right away, and this author like many others obviously takes that advice seriously. (By the way, after reading that first line I put the book back in the bookstore shelf.)

Through the use of computer generated imagery (CGI), many of today's motion pictures follow a similar path, with violent action taking place almost non-stop from the first minute until the credits roll. I enjoy such action movies as much as the next guy, but after a while they all seem to melt into an amorphous blob of mixed memories. Movies, and books, that skillfully blend action with character development and rich settings are far more memorable, and are the more likely candidates for Academy Awards and Pulitzer Prizes.

I look with skepticism on the bang->bang->bang->bang! style of presentation, but there is certainly a market for it and you may want to structure your book as a non-stop series of explosions and gun fights. There's nothing wrong with that, especially if you use evocative words to create memorable characters and scenes along the way. The result can be quite satisfying.

If you intend to follow a more traditional path, keep in mind that no matter what structure you choose, nearly every story has a beginning, middle and end. That's another way of expressing Aristotle's three-act formula.

In general, you may wish to devote the first quarter or so of your novel to introducing and establishing characters and settings and putting conflicts into motion. In the middle section you can recount a series of events to advance the story. In the final quarter the conflicts can be brought to a final crisis, the difficulties resolved and the story brought to an end.

One useful trick to assure your story stays on track is to keep a timeline of events in your plot. If you're one of those who plan ahead, the timeline will be part of your outline. Even for the "cats" that compose on the fly, it's a good idea to keep a running tab of the chain of events as they emerge on the page. This helps keep things in order and makes it easier to identify *plot holes*, those gaps where the reader is denied the knowledge of something they need to know.

Probably the most important words in your story are found in the very first paragraph. That's because if you fail to capture readers right off the bat, they're unlikely to read the rest of your masterpiece. What's the best way to start your story? Well, I wish I could say do *this* and tell you exactly what to write, but truth is hard enough to tell and to create imaginative and effective fiction can be even more difficult than to describe mere reality.

For old time bards it was enough to merely say "Once upon a time..." and people would gather around to hear the story. Things are no longer so easy, and there are perhaps as many ways to start a story as stars in the sky. Some are excellent, others merely meh! and many absolutely dreadful. Your challenge is to create one that is at the very least not awful, and hopefully good or even excellent.

The point of a beginning is to draw the reader immediately into your story. In fact, many critics use the term *hook* to describe the opening passage of a book. Like a master fisherman you want to lure your potential readers to the bait, set the barbs, and begin the careful process of reeling them in. The goal is to catch readers' attention, intrigue them by appealing to their curiosity, and get them to turn the first page.

A common mistake is to include too much description in opening scenes. Let action lead the pace, giving just enough description to suggest the setting.

As always, it helps to study how other authors have addressed this challenge. Here are some examples to ponder:

> It was a bright cold day in April, and the clocks were striking thirteen. – George Orwell, *1984*.

> It was the best of times, it was the worst of times, it was the age of wisdom, it was the age of foolishness, it was the epoch of belief, it was the epoch of incredulity, it was the season of Light, it was the season of Darkness, it was the spring of hope, it was the winter of despair. – Charles Dickens, *A Tale of Two Cities*.

> I had the story, bit by bit, from various people, and, as generally happens in such cases, each time it was a different story. – Edith Wharton, *Ethan Frome*.

> Mr. and Mrs. Dursley, of number four, Privet Drive,

were proud to say that they were perfectly normal, thank you very much. They were the last people you'd expect to be involved in anything strange or mysterious, because they just didn't hold with such nonsense. – J. K. Rowling, *Harry Potter and the Sorcerer's Stone*.

He was an old man who fished alone in a skiff in the Gulf Stream and he had gone eighty-four days now without taking a fish. – Ernest Hemingway, *The Old Man and the Sea*.

Once upon a time, there was a woman who discovered she had turned into the wrong person. – Anne Tyler, *Back When We Were Grownups*.

He was an inch, perhaps two, under six feet, powerfully built, and he advanced straight at you with a slight stoop of the shoulders, head forward, and a fixed from-under stare which made you think of a charging bull. His voice was deep, loud, and his manner displayed a kind of dogged self-assertion which had nothing aggressive in it. It seemed a necessity, and it was directed apparently as much at himself as anybody else. He was spotlessly neat, appareled in immaculate white from shoes to hat, and in the various Eastern ports where he got his living as a ship-chandler's water-clerk he was very popular. – Joseph Conrad, *Lord Jim*.

All children, except one, grow up. – J. M. Barrie, *Peter Pan*.

I am a camera with its shutter open, quite passive, recording, not thinking. – Christopher Isherwood, *Goodbye To Berlin*.

In my younger and more vulnerable years my father gave me some advice that I've been turning over in my mind ever since. Whenever you feel like criticizing any one, he told me, just remember that all the people in this world haven't had the advantages that you've had. – F. Scott Fitzgerald, *The Great Gatsby*.

It was just noon that Sunday morning when the sheriff reached the jail with Lucas Beauchamp though the whole town (the whole county too for that matter) had known since the night before that Lucas had killed a white man. – William Faulkner, *Intruder in the Dust*.

The cold passed reluctantly from the earth, and the retiring fogs revealed an army stretched out on the hills, resting. – Stephen Crane, *The Red Badge of Courage*.

"Well, Prince, Genoa and Lucca are now no more than private estates of the Bonaparte family. No, I warn you, that if you do not tell me we are at war, if you again allow yourself to palliate all the infamies and atrocities of this Antichrist (upon my word, I believe he is), I don't know you in future, you are no longer my friend, no longer my faithful slave, as you say. There, how do you do, how do you do? I see I'm scaring you, sit down and talk to me." – Leo Tolstoy, *War and Peace* (translation).

As Gregor Samsa awoke one morning from uneasy dreams he found himself transformed in his bed into a monstrous vermin. – Franz Kafka, "Metamorphosis" (translation).

The exterior ice chime sounded, warning of potential ice on the roadway, and Gerhard Miner gripped the leather steering wheel of his black Audi A6 a little tighter. His Gucci-clad foot pressed down harder on the accelerator. The sun was setting over Lake Lucerne, and a chill wind, blowing since lunch, began to pick up. Ah, what a lunch that was today, Miner thought to himself as the sleek black sedan hugged the shores of the choppy Swiss lake. It was absolutely exquisite. – Brad Thor, *The Lions of Lucerne*.

It is a truth universally acknowledged, that a single man in possession of a good fortune, must be in want of a wife. – Jane Austen, *Pride and Prejudice*.

Call me Ishmael. – Herman Melville, *Moby Dick*.

And just for fun, here's the opening of one of my own novels:

> The body is displayed on the desert sand like an offering to the gods. It lies on its back, head to the east, feet pointed west. It is the corpse of a man in executive suit, coat buttoned, hands crossed on chest, sightless eyes staring into the blue New Mexico sky. – David L. Brown, *Retirement Man*.

You will recognize many of these opening lines because they are among the best known of their kind. Others are merely ones that happened to come to my attention. And what do they have in common? Perhaps it's that they have little or nothing at all in common, and that very distinction may be their power. Successful beginnings invite readers to travel new-discovered lands. They are the sparkling lures that aim to draw them in and set the hook.

As I've said, stories today don't often begin with the words "Once upon a time..." and yet in a kind of ironic defiance of that rule, one example above does exactly that while presenting a puzzling statement. It works for Ann Tyler, once, but I would not advise you to try it.

Some of these first lines introduce characters ("He was an old man..."; "Call me Ishmael"); settings ("It was the best of times..."); or both ("It was just noon that Sunday morning..."; "The exterior ice chime sounded..."). Others are intended to prompt curiosity. How could a woman turn into the wrong person? Why does the clock strike thirteen? And why would the Dursley's be concerned about anything strange or mysterious?

Do not try to put too much into your beginnings. Ludwig Mies van der Rohe said of architecture, "less is more," and the same can often be applied with good effect to a written work of fiction. In general, opening paragraphs might merely hint at some important fact rather than revealing it, the better to induce curiosity. "Call me Ishmael" with its stark simplicity would no doubt bring a smile to van der Rohe's lips, as would the opening of Peter Pan.

But that doesn't mean a longer opening can't work. Note the Brad Thor paragraph above as an example. The opening paragraph of John Le Carré's novel *Tinker, Tailor, Soldier, Spy* (I won't quote it here) goes on for at least 300 words, a solid mass of gray that flows all the way onto the second page in my paperback edition before finally gasping to a stop.

Remember, the more skillful an author is, the more he or she can pretend there are no rules. Well, hardly any. Long, short, or in-between, it's not the number of words that counts, but the quality of the words, the power they bring to the page by sparking in the minds of the reader images, ideas, feelings, and above all a desire to know more. The successful beginning absolutely reaches out and demands that readers turn that page.

An accomplished writer does not compose a sentence by setting down one letter at a time, or even one word after another like a string of beads. The mind of a writer has evolved far beyond that simplistic model and learned to think and compose in full-blown phrases, sentences and paragraphs. Good writing is not like plodding through a series of muddy puddles, but like a river, carrying the attention of your reader along with it. Each sentence must lead naturally to the next, each paragraph onward in an unbroken flow.

Appropriate *pace*, that is the speed with which your plot advances, is vital to your story. If the pace is too fast, your readers may tire. If too slow, they may lose interest. It's important to change the pace, speeding up for action scenes, slowing down for transitional passages.

Use pace to always advance your story. Avoid the irrelevant. Don't get wrapped up in excessive backstory too early in the narrative. Readers like to know what's going to happen, and are less interested in what happened in the past.

So what next? Well, as some wag once defined history as "one damned thing after another," so your story must move in a connected line of scenes. Your challenge is to introduce your characters, develop them, establish the setting, and set things in motion much as a film director calls out "Action!" You might think of the structure as something like a roller coaster, with scenes rising to crises then swooping down to apparent calm before once again rising to a crescendo of action and bringing you breathless to the exit ramp.

Now I am not suggesting that your novel should consist of a series of scenes strung together on a wire. Far from it. Scenes can introduce mystery, hint at dark dangers, help round out a character, set the stage for some unexpected future event, flash back to some seminal occurrence in the past – all of those and more, as long as each contributes to the continued involvement of the reader in your story, for the story itself is everything. You are the bard, the storyteller, and your job is to entertain and keep the attention of your readers. Never forget that there are no rules, or hardly any, as long as what you create meets those essential ends.

Even after a fine start, sometimes upon reaching the middle of the story a writer feels like a wanderer lost at the edge of a vast desert. It's here that your story may start to lose momentum. This is a sign there isn't enough story to tell, but the solution is at hand. Just add more obstacles, sub-plots, struggles and frustrations for the protagonist. This can carry your story ahead in style.

Always think in terms of how to introduce new challenges to your characters, and in particular the protagonist. You don't want his or her life to be easy, for that would be uninteresting. If you want to craft the maximum in nail-biting, spine-tingling, edge-of-the-seat tension, try to imagine the worst thing that could occur at each point in your story and make it happen. When one problem is resolved, throw out another literary hand grenade. Keep doing this and you will carry the reader along with you. I have seen advice that all novels should be written in just such a way, but that seems like overkill to me (perhaps literally).

In his novella *Candide*, Voltaire's title character is told that he lives in "the best of all possible worlds," only to suffer every imaginable tragedy. Not every story can be Candide's, so it's probably best to back off the throttle a bit and throw in some events that are merely difficult, serious, puzzling, embarrassing, frustrating or inconvenient for the protagonist.

In general, your plot should take the main character or characters from one troubling situation, to something worse, to yet deeper trouble, and so forth until at last, perhaps in the very last chapter when the reader is about to conclude that all is lost, things turn out for the better.

(Or, if you're writing a tragedy, perhaps not so much better as worst of all. In *A Tale of Two Cities*, the final scene involves the imminent decapitation of the hero.)

Now these exciting sequences do not have to involve physical action as seen in shoot-'em-up thrillers. They can be emotional setbacks, threats arising from natural causes such as the danger of thirst, hunger, accident and illness, or even crises brought about by one or more of the Seven Deadly Sins: Lust, Gluttony, Greed, Sloth, Wrath, Envy and Pride.

In fact, those "magnificent seven" are excellent sources of seasoning as you create and launch your characters. Whether attributed to your protagonist, antagonist, or supporting characters, a pinch of lust or a dash of greed will make them seem more like real flesh-and-blood human beings.

* * * * *

Just as opening lines are important to attracting the reader, closing lines are that final touch that will make your book memorable.

Here are a few examples of effective endings:

> So we beat on, boats against the current, borne back ceaselessly into the past. – F. Scott Fitzgerald, *The Great Gatsby*.

> Then starting home, he walked toward the trees, and under them, leaving behind him the big sky, the whisper of wind voices in the wind-beat wheat. – Truman Capote, *In Cold Blood*

> Tomorrow, I'll think of some way to get him back. After all, tomorrow is another day. – Margaret Mitchell, *Gone With the Wind*.

> The offing was barred by a black bank of clouds, and the tranquil waterway leading to the utmost ends of the earth flowed somber under an overcast sky – seemed to lead into the heart of an immense darkness. – Joseph Conrad, *Heart of Darkness*.

> He loved Big Brother. – George Orwell, *1984*.

> He reached the top of the bank in a single, powerful leap. Hazel followed; and together they slipped away, running easily down through the wood, where the first primroses were beginning to bloom. – Richard Adams, *Watership Down*.

> I wrote at the start that this was a record of hate, and walking there beside Henry towards the evening glass of beer, I found the one prayer that seemed to serve the winter mood: O God, You've done enough, You've robbed me of enough, I'm too tired and old to learn to love, leave me alone forever. – Graham Greene, *The End of the Affair*.

A closing is a kind of farewell to the characters your readers will have learned to know, respect, possibly love, hate or admire. It's my thought that an effective ending should not only wrap up the story, but should also, as in most of these examples, hint at continuance, assurance that the characters will continue to act and interact in their imaginary world just as real people lead real lives. It's the author's last chance to convince the reader that the characters have a kind of reality, that sense of rightness that makes for great stories, or even ones that are merely good.

If you want to learn more about how critics and philosophers believe you should organize your book, you may want to read *Structuring Your Novel*, by K.M. Weiland, (available from Amazon and elsewhere). Aristotle's *Poetics* is a basic source on the three-act model (free for Kindle and other e-readers). And, of course, you can Google your way into a world of information from the Internet by typing a few keywords.

Word Power

Chapter Nine

Talking the Talk

Perhaps the greatest challenge to the writer of fiction is when the words you type are intended to come from the mouths of your characters. *Dialog* is the very backbone of almost any story, because it lets us see characters in action. It's through good dialog that you bring them to life, letting the reader discover their goals and desires, quirks and secrets, inner knowledge, biases and opinions.

Here is how it is: What if you lived your life in a world of silence, filled with blank-eyed strangers who never speak. You can observe them, see how they move and dress, what they like to eat, with whom they associate. You can see them engage in actions, appear and disappear at will, sometimes love or be loved, kill or be killed, but never once does a single word pass their frozen lips.

That may give you an idea of how a novel would be without dialog. It would almost certainly be a very dull and uninteresting novel indeed. It might tell a full-blown story, but a two-dimensional one, painted in tones of gray, devoid of character, personality, individual thought – in short, lacking everything that makes stories interesting and worth reading.

Almost all of our experience of human society consists of dialog, the exchange of spoken words. Yes we can learn much by watching others, or sitting in a dark corner reading books, but no true understanding of what it's like to be a human being can be learned without sharing words spoken aloud. Dialog, the spoken words of your characters, should take a prominent place in your memoir or work of fiction.

Your readers want to hear your characters speak, so get down off your soapbox, zip your lips, and let the characters get a word in. A major part of your story should be in the form of dialog, perhaps even half or more of the total lines, with the balance as narrative. When you bring characters to life you owe them the freedom to express themselves, to stand up and walk the walk, and certainly to talk the talk. (Yes, that is still a cliché.)

Once you've created them, let the characters live the story for the readers – and the best way to do that is to let them do your job for you instead of droning on and on about what's happening, what might happen, who's likely to be doing what, and so forth and so on. Nobody wants to listen to you – they're waiting to hear from your characters. They're the stars of your show. Get out of their way and let them tell their stories. You're the director in the wings, not the actor on the stage.

Dialog should be dramatic, even melodramatic, but never to excess. Let your dialog rise in emotional pitch to create tension or highlight conflict. But drama can be built without unleashing a flood of florid prose. Sometimes a single word of dialog, or even silence, can add tension. like this:

"I love you," Mary said.
Bob looked away and made no reply.

Don't tell us what Bob's thinking – let him tell it himself through his actions Or use dialog to help him try to explain himself to Mary, or even himself on a lonely beach in the form of internal dialog or soliloquy. Don't describe how Rachel falls into the well – have her cry out for help, express her thanks to her rescuers, and explain to her mother why she was in the old orchard.

Writing dialog is a difficult craft, for it requires you to give up your own diction, word choices and world view and substitute those of your characters. You cannot have them all speak and think the same, or they will come off like a display of department store mannequins. Nor should they all sound like you.

Each character will reveal facets of themselves through their speech. By the words you give them you can bring them to a literary semblance of life. If your character is a pirate, he might talk like a pirate (*arrh*!). If a cowboy, why shucks, he needs to talk that way. If she's a stuck up Southern Belle, she draws out her vowels as if looking down her nose at you ("why bless your dear little heart"). If he's a tough man of action, his language should reflect that ("fill your hand, you son of a bitch"). Of course, your characters should not sound exactly like Long John Silver, Scarlett O'Hara or Rooster Cogburn, since those characters have already become clichés.

Here's another take on the challenge of writing good dialog, according to surgeon-turned-writer William H. Coles:

> In great fiction, dialogue is not intuitive, and it does not come naturally to writers. Most importantly, for effective dialogue in fiction, authors cannot simply describe a dialogue from real experience or from an imagined scene. Basically, dialogue is always created for the purpose of story development, therefore, it cannot function as a taped recording of reality; and it must be stripped of nuances that may not be true to the story or confuse the reader. In revision of dialogue, these questions are useful: Is dialogue logical? Does it fit character desire and motivation? Does it support theme and meaning? Does it move?

As mentioned in an earlier chapter, characters don't need to speak in complete sentences as if they were diagramming them on a Middle School whiteboard. Real people don't talk that way. No, they don't. At least, not all the time, and neither should your characters. They can stammer, interrupt each other, lose track of their trains of thought, and utter meaningless words such as "umm," or "gee" (but not to excess).

A real person might seldom say "yes," preferring such alternatives as *yep, yeah, sho 'nuf, ya got that right.* Instead of "no," they might say *nope, nah, ain't that bad,* or *butt out.*

If they're from some foreign land they might use such words as *ja, nein, nyet, non,* or *si.* If they're poorly educated they will likely use improper grammar, use incorrect words (this is known as malapropism), or sprinkle their English with expletives. If a member of a sub-culture (Black ghetto, Jewish, Hispanic) they will likely use idioms of their cultures.

It helps to have an ear for language, and using dialog effectively may be one of the hardest tasks you face as a writer. Try to focus on listening to spoken language when out and about in public. The way you hear English spoken out there in the real world is the real language, the true words of power when it comes to writing dialog. To bring your characters to life on the page, listen and learn to apply the myriad ways real people speak.

But here's an important caveat: Do not overdo this or your dialog will turn into a mess of verbal garbage. As in all things, less is more. Use dialog quirks sparingly, just enough to cue the reader. When you use too much seasoning in your dialog, you will almost certainly spoil the dish.

When crafting dialog, remember these common mistakes:

- Don't use dialog merely to break up a long narrative passage. If the story seems to be dragging, address the narrative problem instead of trying to cover it up with an injection of witty repartee from a character. Make sure the narrative is flowing and the problem will take care of itself. (On the other side of this coin, see the description below about how to blend narrative with dialog,)

• Never write static prose as dialog. Characters must sound like real people, not literary essayists.

• Avoid dialog that has no purpose in advancing the story. For example, directing characters to chat about the weather or sports scores just to fill space. That will turn off readers in fiction just as it does in real life.

• Never let dialog slow down the action. When bullets are flying it's no time for characters to start blathering at each other as in this silly example:

> "What was that noise?"
> "I think someone's shooting at us."
> "Gosh, I think you're right. Look, isn't that a bullet hole in the tree beside you?"
> "Looks like it. Do you think it's a nine millimeter?"
> "I'd say a forty-five."
> "Yeah, you're probably right. That's some serious firepower."

Don't do that. Keep the narrative going, because it's always through narrative, not dialog, that action can be portrayed.

• Never write dialog that tells the reader something they already know. When John tells Mary what happened to him during the riot, and his experience has already been told as narrative, don't bore the reader by having him repeat it all in his words. Better to say something like this: John told Mary what had happened. Then, with that out of the way, you can use dialog to report Mary's reaction and keep the story moving forward

• Similarly, avoid using dialog for one character to inform another of something he or she already knows. For example, it would be silly for John to say: "Mary, remember when we were lost in the woods last year and were almost eaten by that grizzly bear?" Chances are that unless she's suffering from amnesia or Alzheimer's disease Mary does remember, so the dialog sounds off-key. If the reader needs to be informed of something the characters already know, do it through narrative, perhaps by using flashback to the earlier episode.

• Don't use dialog that might be perceived as commentary by the author. It is very important to remember that your characters are not you. They must live and act out their own separate (if imagined) lives. Never allow your personal tastes, biases or opinions to come from a character unless those traits have been established as belonging to that character. Furthermore, the insight must advance the action or help develop the character.

Of course, you may share qualities with the character, but you must first give them to him or her before they can express them in a way that is true for them. This is a subtle concept that requires a bit of thinking, but it is important because successful authors must keep their characters in focus and avoid interposing themselves in the character's thoughts and actions.

• Don't make your characters use each other's names frequently, as in this extreme example:

"Mary, what are we having for dinner?"
"Why John, we're having braised short ribs
   with rice and carrots."
"Oh, Mary, you know that's my favorite."
"Yes, John, I know."

That's not the way real people talk, and neither should your characters. They are allowed to use the names of their companions at the beginning of a scene, and for dramatic purpose ("Oh, my God, Mary, what's happened?") but otherwise frequent naming should be avoided.

• When you as the author need to establish who is speaking and to whom, do so in the attribution following the character's line (i.e. John said.). But don't overdo that, either. In most instances, once the characters are identified *he* and *she* are the preferred identifying labels, and even those can be skipped as long as it's clear who the speakers are.

• Following up on the last point, be sure that it's always clear which character is speaking. There is a best-selling writer of thrillers who often fails at that, by this formula: First character A speaks, then character B speaks or acts in some way. In the next paragraph the author refers to "he" or "she" speaking or acting, but in reference to A, not B as one would suppose. This causes a moment of confusion on the part of the reader.

As that example illustrates, the problem can most often arise with the use of pronouns, where the antecedent is unclear. When in doubt, remind the reader clearly of the antecedent to which the pronoun refers. This can be done by replacing the pronoun with the character's name or a descriptive label ("the detective," "the young woman," "the priest," "the warrior" and so forth).

• Avoid direct answers to a question that do not advance the action. For example:

> "Is that a Blackhawk helicopter coming our way?"
> "Yes, that's a Blackhawk helicopter."

This example is wrong on several levels. Of course, it utterly fails to advance the action. Also, the question is lacking in emotional content, almost like a comment on the nice weather or how good the coffee tastes. Bland, meaningless blather does nothing to create conflict and crisis that will make readers yearn to find out what's going to happen next. A better response would be something along the lines of: "Oh my god, I think you're right!"

• Don't let your characters sound like talking heads on the evening news. A conversation should always include elements of conflict or surprise, divulge new information, reveal a secret, develop a logical thread that contributes to the plot, and anything else that helps keep the story moving.

• Provide reaction from others when one character is the main speaker. If the lead character is making statements and the other merely agreeing through inane responses such as *yes, of course, I see, yep* or *you're right*, it's going to bore the reader and that is never a good thing. Such dialog is not interesting and does not create conflict or action. The content would probably best be told through narrative rather than having the speaker ramble on.

• I have extolled the virtues of analogy, but dialog is usually not the place for metaphors or similes. People tend to speak in direct terms, and figures of speech are best reserved for narrative (and never to be overused even then). There are exceptions, for example when a speaker is attempting to explain a concept and an analogy helps him or her get the point across. However, as pointed out earlier, it's okay to have your characters use clichés.

• Make sure that the dialog matches the intellectual, cultural and educational background of the character. As mentioned earlier in this chapter, when they speak characters must sound like the kind of person they are. Thugs must speak like thugs, lawyers like lawyers, waitresses like waitresses and Navy SEALs like Navy SEALs (*Hooyah!*), for if they don't no one will believe in them. It's vital that the reader can relate to your characters or they will have no interest in what happens to them.

You can begin to develop your own how-to list by taking the reverse of many of the "rules" listed above; in other words, doing the opposite of what is warned against. Here are some further suggestions:

• Don't be too formal. As noted above, real people don't talk like English teachers.

• On the other side, don't be too realistic. By that I mean making the dialog sound like a transcript including every uh, um, hesitation and mistaken word. Neither should your cowboy or lawyer use so many unfamiliar words, jargon and strange pronunciations that it becomes a garbled mess incomprehensible to most readers. Remember: A little bit of spice is nice; too much spoils the dish.

• Don't overuse a variety of words to identify the tone of a statement. By that, I mean using words such as *she screamed, he shouted, she admonished*, and so forth. Not that there is anything wrong with those verbs, it's just that too much of anything becomes tiresome.

There are critics and writers who believe that only the word "said" should be used when attributing a line of dialog. Others don't go quite so far but recommend limiting it to *said, asked, answered,* and perhaps the occasional *whispered.* I cannot agree with these extreme limitations. English provides us with a wide palette of verbs to refer to speech, and we should use them, although sparingly and only when appropriate. If characters are always shouting and screaming and accusing each other, the readers will come to view them like "the little boy who cried wolf." Note that in that cliché the boy did not just *say* "wolf," he *cried* it. If he had only said it he would perhaps have lived to a ripe old age.

When a dramatic reading is given, the presenter raises and lowers his or her voice, introduces dramatic pauses, and so forth. The voice is used to give power to the words, to simulate the way they might have been spoken should the characters be real live people. Similarly, through the choice of verb to attribute a line of dialog you can add emphasis, emotion, and drama to your characters' lines. Consider these alternatives:

"Oh, no," she said.
"Oh, no," she replied with a smile.
"Oh, no," she remarked casually.
"Oh, no," she denied modestly.
"Oh, no," she pleaded in desperation.
"Oh, no," she cried in surprise.
"Oh, no," she blurted.

"Oh, no," she breathed sensually.
"Oh, no," she sputtered nervously.
"Oh, no," she announced with a frown.
"Oh, no," she remarked sarcastically.
"Oh, no," she argued.
"Oh, no," she murmured despondently.

Notice that the choice of verb makes the simple two-word statement serve a variety of very different purposes. Also, by adding an adverb (*casually, modestly, nervously, sarcastically*) you can add yet another layer of meaning to the words.

As always, use alternates sparingly. Good old *said* (or, in its present tense form *says*) is probably best most of the time, but it's nice to have a full range of tools in your toolbox, ready to add that little touch of extra meaning that makes good writing work.

And for goodness sakes, make sure your dialog tags make sense. To write, "Here I am," Bob smiled, makes no sense. Smiling is not speaking.

• Not all conversations need to be written out word-for-word. Sometimes it works better and keeps the action moving if the conversation is summarized as narrative. If two characters talk for two hours about whether or not to rob the train, we probably don't have to learn every detail but merely the conclusion. Example: "After a long, contentious argument around the campfire, Bob gives in and agrees to help Jim rob the train." The action moves on.

• Use weird spellings sparingly. It can add a touch of spice to have your character say *shore* instead of *sure*, or *dunno* instead of *don't know*, but as with most things in good writing, too much can be a turnoff to readers.

• In general, it's a good idea to break up dialog with narrative. I once wrote a critique of a novel in which several long speeches were included in the storyline. The author presented them as if they were transcripts. The character did not pause to turn the page or look around nor did the audience move or react in any way. In fact, one chapter was titled "The President's Speech," and that's exactly what it was, no more and no less. If you want to put your readers to sleep, this is a good way to do it.

Yes, I know that in *Atlas Shrugged* Ayn Rand gave John Galt an 80-page speech in which he laid out his (actually Rand's) political and economic ideas virtually non-stop (a violation of the point made above about not letting the author's thoughts get into a character's mouth), but that's a famous exception with which many critics find fault.

• It's always better to intersperse some narrative when asking characters to engage in long conversations. You may have them clear their throat, pause to light a cigar, get up and walk around, look out the window to check for snipers, start cleaning their pistol, stroke the cat's ears or just about anything that people do in the course of ordinary events. By sprinkling your characters' dialog with narrative actions you'll make the scene more interesting and real to the reader. It can also give you a chance to develop individual character traits.

Here's an example of dialog and narrative blended smoothly together, lines I picked almost at random from the first book that came to hand, Tony Hillerman's novel

The Blessing Way. Navajo Tribal Policeman Joe Leaphorn is investigating a death in the desert:

> ...Leaphorn walked suddenly to the nearest bush and examined it. He motioned to Roanhorse, and McKee followed.
> "You pull a limb off this for anything?"
> Roanhorse shook his head.
> There was a raw wound where a limb had been broken away. Leaphorn put his thumb against the exposed cambium layer and showed it to McKee. It was sticky with fresh sap.
> "What do you think of that?"
> "Nothing," McKee said. "How about you?"
> "I don't know. Probably nothing."
> He started walking back toward the body, through the creosote bush, searching. Bitsi, McKee noticed, had climbed back into the carryall.
> "Look around across the road there," Leaphorn said, "and see if you can find that juniper branch."
> But he found it himself. The frail needles were dirty and broken. McKee guessed it had been used as a broom even before Leaphorn told him.
> "That looked pretty smart, Joe," McKee said. "Where does it take you?"
> "I don't know." Leaphorn was looking intently at the body...

Always keep in mind that dialog must never be used for its own sake, but only to help shape your characters, create conflict, inform the reader of things they need to know, and move the story ahead without hesitation, in this case the discovery of a clue.

Here's another example, from my own murder mystery *Retirement Man.* Posing as a freelance writer, private detective Rob

Charlton is about to meet a retired French chef who may have information about a case Charlton is investigating.

The door opens and Bisset bustles into the room. A portly gentleman of about 80 he looks the part of an aging but well-fed chef, with extra chins and a round belly. His hair's gray but his blue eyes are bright and piercing. He shakes my hand and guides me to the little tasting table. I offer one of my freelance writer cards and take a seat.

He sits down opposite me and smiles. He's actually beaming. I'm reminded of statues of the Laughing Buddha, round and filled with jollity. Goodness, I've seldom felt so welcome. Without asking he pours wine into a glass and places it in front of me. He pours for himself and raises his glass.

"As you know, *monsieur*, wine is very important to we French people. There is an old saying in my country, '*Un jour sans vin est comme un jour sans soleil*'. It means in English 'A day without the wine is like a day without the sunshine'. Thank heavens for *le vin*, for without it we could not be French, *oui*?"

We click glasses and I take a sip. It's excellent, rich with flavor and without the bitter aftertaste of so many of the everyday bottles I buy at Marv's.

"And so we also enjoy *le pain*, or as you call it, bread, the staff of life," Bisset continues, tearing off a piece of the loaf and handing it to me. "This came from my oven just before a half hour," he adds.

Indeed the bread is still warm and tastes delightful. He cuts a wedge of cheese and for a moment I enjoy the wine-and-cheese treat. Maybe there's something to this French cuisine stuff. Bisset watches me, his face wreathed in smiles, delighting in my pleasure. With his infectious love for food and drink I can begin to see why he was such a successful restaurateur.

In a few brief paragraphs I've introduced a minor character and shown a reminder of Charlton's ordinary taste in food (he loves biscuits and gravy and bacon cheeseburgers). Narrative and dialog are blended smoothly. Bisset's lines are sprinkled with words and phrases from his native French, but without overdoing it. Note that it's written in first person and present tense. I talked about that in Chapter 5.

> • Finally, it's usually a good idea to use contractions in dialog. (Rule: It ain't bad to use contractions.) It sounds a lot more like the way real people talk when your character says: "Bob isn't the one; he couldn't have done it," rather than "Bob is not the one; he could not have done it." This relates to the item above about not making your characters speak in too formal a way (unless they are English teachers or robots). Axiom: Robots don't talk like real people. Reason: they're not. Lesson: Your human characters should never talk like robots.

Let's move on to the subject of how to create and maintain action and make your story flow like a river.

Chapter Ten

Walking the Walk

Now that you've established your characters and settings, it's time to start the story rolling. As the movie director says: "lights, camera, action!" This is where the hard part comes, because for your novel or memoir you must be that director to make your story unfold. Just as cinema actors must stay on their roles, speak their lines well and as intended by the script, and move about the set without stumbling over the odd lighting cable, you must keep your cast on track to tell your story.

It's all about *action*.

Now before we go any deeper into this subject, let's be clear that action can be anything that changes the situation. It does not have to involve the physical, for it can be a realization by a character, a thought expressed in dialog, a natural event such as a thunderstorm or blizzard, even small things such as a loud noise, the scent of gunpowder, or the touch of a bitter wind on the protagonist's cheek. It can be the receipt of a message, the sound of someone at the window, or the roar of a wild beast in the nearby jungle.

As you can deduce from this, there are major actions, minor actions, and what I like to call mini-actions. The point is that the story must continue to flow, and it is through action that your story unfolds. You are like a steam-train engineer, and once your engine leaves the station you must keep it moving to the destination. You do this through a continuous thread of actions large and small. Actions in a narrative are like the lumps of coal shoveled into the engine's firebox. (See how analogy can create mind pictures to make a point?)

Your choices of actions are crucial to the success of your story. If you inject too many major actions in your plot, the effect can be overwhelming. On the other hand, spend too much time on mini-actions and your readers are likely to become bored and (gasp!) fail to turn the page.

The worst thing you can do is bore your reader. *New Yorker* cartoonist Tom Gauld tells how not to do it by describing the "Four Undramatic Plot Structures":

> 1. The hero is confronted by an antagonistic force and ignores it until it goes away.
>
> 2. The protagonist is accused of wrongdoing, but it's not a big thing and soon gets sorted out.
>
> 3. The heroine is faced with a problem but it's really difficult so she gives up.
>
> 4. A man wants something. Later, he's not so sure. By suppertime he's forgotten all about it.

There are two dangers a writer faces when crafting a novel. One is to have a "soft" middle. This may seem surprising, but it is a common problem. The writer has a good idea to start out with, and a whale of a good ending – but what about that vast number of words that need to go in between?

Another danger is to leave gaps in the story, what critics call *plot holes.* This confuses the reader and causes her to say "Huh?" You don't want your readers to do that, any more than you want them to be bored.

These dangers are less likely to appear if you keep the story moving with a continuing thread of actions, all tied together in a logical timeline.

Perhaps the important rule here is that no action should be introduced unless it moves the story in some way. It may reveal information, change a character's ideas or expectations, turn the protagonist's world completely upside down, or merely emphasize a character trait by, for example, having him turn down the offer of a cigarette, having her mention that she's a divorcee, or describe the antagonist's love of firearms.

All these things taken together are the building blocks, timbers, bricks, mortar, windowpanes and doors that make up the structure of your story. Action is like the gasoline that makes your car run, the wind that drives the rain, or the Louisville Slugger the batter uses to drive the ball into the stands.

It is *force*, and to be effective it requires the power of words.

As with every phase of writing, the words are the key. If written poorly, the most imaginative and amazing action scene will fail to entrance the reader. On the other hand, everyday scenes such as a group at a dinner table can be compelling.

Here's an excerpt from my novel *Sarah and the Dragon* that illustrates this point. Sarah has become a student of the dragon Dar-Agoné (an ancient alien). After having disappeared for several weeks being taught by the Dragon, she's connected with Air Force Col. John Spencer and returns to her parent's house in California with Spencer in tow.

> They go inside where dinner awaits. They sit in a large
> dining room and a housekeeper serves the meal before

139

withdrawing. Spencer's seated away from the others, at the far end of the long table. Sarah sits at her father's right, facing her mother across the table. Her father pours rich red wine in their glasses and proposes a toast.

"Here's to you, Colonel," he says, raising his glass, "for rescuing and bringing our daughter back to us."

Spencer clears his throat and keeps his glass on the table.

"Sir, you should know your daughter brought me here, not the other way around."

The parents stare at him for a moment then turn their eyes to Sarah who seems to be struggling to hold in a smile.

"What do you mean?" her father asks.

"Oh, you'll see," Spencer remarks, raising his glass. "But I'll drink a toast. Here's to Sarah."

They raise their glasses then pass around pot roast, creamed baby potatoes with fresh peas, hot rolls and a light salad with avocado slices and red onion rings. Sarah takes the largest servings of all and is the first to help herself to seconds.

As the server clears the table her mother begins to speak.

"Sarah, we're so glad you're back with us," she proclaims. "Your room is just the same as ever..."

"Well, gosh, Mom," Sarah breaks in. "I don't know why not, since I've only been gone about a month."

Her equilibrium disturbed, her mother dithers a moment before picking up her thread.

"Honey," she says quietly, "please forgive me. You have to realize we thought you were dead, that we'd never see you again."

"Oh, right Mom. I'm sorry. Please go on." Sarah wonders if her mother had ideas of renting out her room. She keeps the thought to herself.

"You've got a lot to do," her mother lectures her. "It's only a few weeks until you start at Harvard..."

"Mom, I'm not going to Harvard."

There's a short silence. Spencer's watching for the explosion, and sure enough it comes.

"What!" Her father roars, slapping his napkin down on the table. "Young lady, do you know what you're saying?"

"Yeah. I said I'm not going to Harvard."

"But... What about your career," her mother blurts out.

"I already have a career," Sarah informs them with a smile.

That leaves them in silence again and Spencer uses his own napkin to cover the smile that comes to his lips. Sarah picks up the wine bottle and pours the last inch into her glass. As she takes a sip her father comes back with a second wave attack.

"Do you know how hard it was to get you that appointment at Harvard?" he demands. "How many lunches with influential Harvard alums, how many pleas to get letters of recommendation, how much..."

"Hey, Dad, cool it," Sarah interjects. "It's not all about you. My near perfect SATs and four-point-oh grade average had something to do with it. Why do you think I was also accepted at Princeton, and with scholarships at both schools? Did you pull strings there, too?"

Her father's flabbergasted. Enraged, he starts to stand up but meets Spencer's steady gaze and quickly sits down again.

"I never asked you to apply at Princeton...," he grumbles.

The setting of this scene is simply one of characters sharing a dinner. Sarah has come to introduce her parents to the fact that her life has been changed forever, and to win over their support. A simple and mundane setting, and yet, the action is palpable.

In this excerpt there are several methods in play. Narrative and dialog are blended to keep the story moving. Characters perform little mini-actions during the sequence (serving food and wine; drinking a toast; fumbling with napkins). Characters speak and act in believable ways – the parents attempting to reassert their dominance; Sarah a bit rebellious in her important new role; Spencer a quiet observer. There are a few general details that help set the scene (a long table; mention of the menu items).

Taken as a whole, this scene could almost be considered as a major action, demonstrating how smaller actions can be placed together to create a larger overall effect. Mini-actions can be used to build encompassing wholes that emerge as minor or even major actions, key turning points in the story.

So now we've seen a bit of how actions carry a story on their back, and how every scene should contain a series of actions of every size. Now let's take a look at truly major actions, those defining events in a story – the times when the monster really is trampling Tokyo; when the protagonist is dodging a sniper's bullets; or the grizzly bear is closing in on the heroine, her foot caught in a crevice.

As mentioned above, major actions should be used sparingly. In general, a major action should take place fairly early in the story, the precipitating event that starts the story rolling. Perhaps the protagonist is faced with a difficult situation – her sabotaged car plummets off the road; he struggles with a bearded man with a knife; her daughter is kidnapped from the school yard; the school is destroyed by a tornado or earthquake; a SWAT team breaks into his office and shoots his secretary; the airplane loses power and spirals out of control. The possibilities for disaster are almost endless.

When writing a major action scene, *time* is of the essence. You must speed things up and slow them down at the same time. Does that seem impossible? What I mean is that although things may be happening really fast (a car crash, knife fight, airplane crash), you can expand time so that readers can absorb the events taking place.

When everything's on the line, it's obviously no time to hesitate. As the old cliché goes, when the going gets tough, the tough get going – and so it is with your major action sequence. The scene must unfold almost second-by-second, with non-stop movement.

Here's an example, from Stephen Hunter's novel *Time to Hunt*. We pick it up just after protagonist Bob Lee Swagger makes a desperate sniper shot through a wooden cellar door to take out a killer who is about to murder Swagger's wife and daughter. The scene shifts to the wife's point of view.

> The pistol settled down; she saw the hugeness of its bore just feet away from her and then felt–
>
> Splatter in her face, a sense of mist or fog suddenly filling the air, a meaty vapor.
>
> Mixed into this sensation was a sound which was that of wood splitting
>
> In it too was a grunt, almost involuntary, as if lungs gurgled, somehow human.
>
> She found herself wet with droplets that proved to be warm and heavy: blood.
>
> The sniper transfigured before her. What had been the upper quadrant of his face had somehow been pulped, ripped open, revealing a terrible wound of splintered bone and spurting blood. One eye looked dead as a nickel; the other was gone in the mess. Even as these details were fixing themselves in her memory, he fell sideways with a thump, his head banging on the cement floor, exposing the ragged entry wound in the corresponding rear quadrant of the skull, where the bones now seemed broken and frail.

A single light beam came through the cellar door where the bullet had passed.

She looked down, saw the stumpy little man fallen like a white angel into a red pool, as his satiny blood spread ever wider from his ruined face.

She turned to her daughter and her friend, who regarded her with their mouths agape, and horror, more than relief registering in both their eyes.

Then she spoke with perfect deliberation:

"Daddy's home."

The words are powerful, bringing the scene to life in all its gory detail. There are short sentences mixed with longer ones; earthy words filled with imagery; an appeal to all the senses. The action may last only two or three seconds, yet Hunter's words fill nearly a full page of narrative, then crashes to a close with two words of dialog that could have come from a 1950's "Leave It to Beaver" TV show. The contrast is striking. Through her words Hunter is telling us that we can start to breathe again.

It's generally not a good idea to burden the reader with too many details, but you can make an exception when describing major actions. These are defining events in your story and you want to make them as real as possible. In this excerpt Hunter invokes the scent and feel of blood, the sounds of the shot and the dying killer's reaction, the sight of his ruined body. There is simile ("like a white angel") and imagery as a single beam of light marks the passage of a bullet through a wooden door. Try to imagine a movie scene as powerful as the words Hunter crafted. You are not merely a neutral observer, but are drawn into the action in a way that only words of power can achieve.

When leading your reader through an intense major action scene, it's a good idea to use short, punchy words, drawn mostly from the center of the word target and the first ring. That's because you don't want your readers to be distracted by unfamiliar words just when you want them to be caught up in your action scene. It can be effective to use short, perhaps telegraphic sentences to keep the event moving – unless you can craft longer sentences that keep the action moving. The choice is yours. There are no rules.

Here's another example of how powerful words can create worlds from mere strokes on a keyboard, from the writer William Gibson's 1984 science fiction novel *Neuromancer*. Gibson coined the term cyberspace and in this scene the protagonist is in a matrix-like world beyond the boundaries of reality, attacking Tessier-Ashpool, a powerful artificial intelligence.

> His mouth filled with an aching taste of blue.
>
> His eyes were eggs of unstable crystal, vibrating with a frequency whose name was rain and the sound of trains, suddenly sprouting a forest of hair-fine glass spines. The spines split, bisected, split again, exponential growth under the dome of the Tessier-Ashpool ice.
>
> The roof of his mouth cleaved painlessly, admitting rootlets that whipped around his tongue, hungry for the taste of blue, to feed the crystal forest of his eyes, forests that pressed against the green dome, pressed and here hindered, and spread, growing down, filling the universe of T-A, down into the waiting, hapless suburbs of the city that was the mind of Tessier-Ashpool S.A.
>
> And he was remembering an ancient story, a king placing coins on a chessboard, doubling the amount at each square.
>
> Exponential.
>
> Darkness fell in from every side, a sphere of singing black, pressure on the extended crystal nerves of the universe of data he had nearly become...

Gibson was challenged to describe a world of bits and bytes, and to do so he wove his words to reflect the strangeness. Taste becomes color; a frequency has a name and the name is rain; the

AI is a city protected by "hapless suburbs." The character is in danger of being transformed irretrievably into data, absorbed forever into the matrix. Strange world indeed, and the images Gibson invokes are not to be taken literally, but to underline the strangeness. Gibson's words make the unimaginable come to life in this action scene.

I showed this quote to a friend, and her comment was "I don't see it," meaning that she couldn't visualize the fictional world of *Neuromancer*. Well, that's the point really – Gibson used words of power to create an imagined setting outside the framework of our ordinary existences. He makes us stretch our minds by crafting images that seem discordant to us, and thus gives us the feeling of visiting a different dimension.

There are two other terms relating to action: *rising action* and *falling action*. Rising action is the narrative episode that leads the reader into a major action; falling action is the resolution of the conflict. This model could be visualized as like a mountain, rising on one side to a snow-covered peak that represents the major action itself, then falling away into a valley beyond.

Major and even some minor actions cannot take place in a vacuum – the background must be laid out in advance, and repercussions dealt with in the aftermath. We've visited these concepts in Chapter 7.

Finally, your narrative is sure to include one singular action that is the culmination of the story – the goal the protagonist strives to reach; the threat that's overcome at last; the emotional crisis to which the entire narrative builds.

We might call this the *peak action*. Thus, if your storyline is drawn as a chart it might resemble a roller coaster and the peak action is the final thrill ride segment. Everything else creates and builds excitement, curiosity, and engagement of the reader to lead him or her to this defining event. The example above from the Stephen Hunter novel is a peak event, the moment toward which the entire book led.

To summarize:
- Actions are the driving forces of your story.
- Major actions are best told using narrative with minimum or no dialog.
- There are major actions, minor actions and mini-actions.
- Effective scenes are built from a series of actions, large and small.
- Your story should contain a singular peak action.
- Slow down and compress time to make actions come to life.
- Consider using simple words and short sentences to narrate actions.
- Remember that rules exist only in the minds of those who create them.

Word Power

David L. Brown

Chapter Eleven

Doing It with Style

As we know, words can have many meanings. It's true of that everyday word *style* so often encountered in connection with the written word. There are several kinds of style, and it pays to know the difference.

One you will often encounter is the idea of a set of strict rules that must be followed in writing for a particular purpose. For example, the Associated Press Stylebook prescribes how a news report must be written in order to be acceptable to the wire service and its subscribers. It dictates which words and phrases can be used or are forbidden; how to spell certain words or names when there are alternatives; when to capitalize and when not to; and so forth.

Stylebooks of this kind are necessary to bring consistency to large volumes of written works being produced by a number of different people. They are like the music sheets followed by every member of a symphony orchestra and without which they would produce a cacophony of noise. It's like programming robots to perform the same tasks.

There are many such stylebooks, including those for individual publications such as *The New York Times Manual of Style and Usage*. For writers of scholarly papers, textbooks and grant proposals, *The*

Chicago Manual of Style from the University of Chicago Press is the go-to resource.

As a writer of fiction, you do not need to pay too much attention to these, but there are certain common conventions that should be incorporated into your writing as a matter of course.

Another meaning for the word style is to describe the individual approach of a particular artist. For example, one might say that someone acts in the style of Sir John Gielgud, sings in the style of Patsy Cline, or paints in the style of Grandma Moses.

In the same way the writing style of an author can often be recognized due to his or her choice of words, rhythm, use of figures of speech, and many other factors. In other words, the way in which the writer employs the many tools we've discussed in earlier chapters – plus some mysterious additional ingredients that come straight out of their hoard of experience and discoveries.

Unlike journalistic stylebooks meant to create sameness, these forms of style indicate differentness. That sort of style cannot be learned from a book but must come from within. It can be the mark of an accomplished writer of power.

Unfortunately, a "recognizable style" can also be a sign of a clumsy and inept writer. Every writer of any consequence has a personal style; it comes with the territory. The challenge is to create your own style that is unique, effective, and versatile enough to allow your story to be told in the best possible way.

Style should be almost invisible, never obvious or intrusive, lest it come between you and your reader. Avoid copycat style that is out-of-date, florid, minimalist, or academic. These are self-indulgent and can only turn off many readers.

Check your exposition against your dialog – if the way your characters speak has a different tone from that of the author it can create a discordant effect. This point is particularly important in first person form where the character acts as narrator and speaks dialog. Take care not to give your characters split personalities, because it will make them seem artificial and contrived.

There is a marvelous little book that every serious writer should keep close at hand. Known to generations of authors and journalists simply as "Strunk and White," its actual title is *The Elements of Style*. It contains a review of standard rules similar to those found in journalistic stylebooks, produced by the late William Strunk, a professor of English at Cornell University. Strunk provides advice on the first kind of style described above.

More importantly to us as creative writers is a chapter by E. B. White, long-time contributor to *The New Yorker* and author of *Charlotte's Web* and *Stuart Little*. White provides insight into the second kind of style, that which makes the work of an individual writer stand out from the ordinary.

Here's how White approaches the subject of style in fine writing:

> Style is an increment in writing. When we speak of Fitzgerald's style, we don't mean his command of the relative pronoun, we mean the sound his words make on paper. Every writer, by the way he uses the language, reveals something of his spirit, his habits, his capacities, his bias. This is inevitable as well as enjoyable. All writing is communication; creative writing is communication through revelation – it is the Self escaping into the open. No writer long remains incognito.

Although it contradicts my earlier admonition about keeping yourself outside of your characters, in a general sense White's point that the personality of the author inevitably colors his or her writing is certainly true. The challenge is to learn how to tap into those inner springs of individuality and craft words of power to express them, while continuing to remain apart like the director in the wings. That's the hard part, the part that requires you first to have unusual talent and then to have read at least a thousand good books and written a million words. Exquisite style is the secret craft of the master writer.

We have much to learn from White's advice. To study more from him, buy a copy of "Strunk and White" and read his chapter titled "An Approach to Style". I will steal no more of his words except to leave you with one more paragraph of White's wisdom on the subject of literary style:

> Young writers often suppose that style is a garnish for the meat of prose, a sauce by which a dull dish is made palatable. Style has no such separate entity; it is nondetachable, unfilterable. The beginner should approach style warily, realizing that it is himself he is approaching, no other, and he should begin by turning resolutely away from all devices that are popularly believed to indicate style – all mannerisms, tricks, adornments. The approach to style is by way of plainness, simplicity, orderliness, sincerity.

As Virginia Woolf once wrote: "Every secret of a writer's soul, every experience of his life, every quality of his mind, is written large in his works."

In other words, you cannot achieve a personal style by rote, through parroting the styles of others, or by merely sprinkling patterns of clever word twists among your paragraphs like flowers strewn along a muddy path. You first must fill yourself with knowledge of the world and of yourself then allow that which you have discovered to come forth through your written words.

Literary style is a subjective thing and hard to define. For meaningful communications to take place, words must mean the same thing to both writer and reader. It's your challenge to craft words that pluck the right tunes on the reader's intellectual and emotional strings.

The twentieth century philosopher Ludwig Wittgenstein devoted much thought to the meaning of words, expressing his belief that mere words are inadequate to fully communicate many abstract or complicated subjects. He wrote: "Little that is meaningful can be said about such matters, they can only be shown."

To demonstrate his point, Wittgenstein wrote of a courtroom procedure in which model cars were used to show the events of an accident. Words were deemed inadequate to fully inform the jury about what took place.

On a philosophical level, Wittgenstein may be correct that complex concepts can only be shown, not built from words. This idea is contained in the old saying about a picture being worth a thousand words. But do not despair, for in the hands of a master words can have power to create realities far beyond what mere pictures can evoke.

Pictures are good at portraying simple concepts, but only words can explore the full panoply of meaning.

Think of Edgar Munch's famous painting "The Scream," that iconic image that glimpses fear and madness. It has a power of sorts, but when you think about it, like all pictures on paper or canvas its power is of a two-dimensional kind.

If drawn with words instead of the medium of paints and canvas, we could learn far more about the subject. The writer could take us inside the mind of the screamer, tell us how he came to be on the wharf, describe the sweat running down his neck, tap into the emotional stress of the moment, yield up the sound of the wind and the scent of the sea, relate the cause of the orange sky that seems to reflect the scream itself, tell what awful vision has caused the subject's eyes to open wide in horror, evoke the feeling of palms pressed over ears as if to block out some terrifying sound....

I could go on and on, because while a picture is bound by the edges of its frame, there are no limits to the power of words.

Let us explore through demonstration that which makes some writing exceptional. Here is a quotation from Thomas Wolfe's novel *You Can't Go Home Again*:

> All things belonging to the earth will never change – the leaf, the blade, the flower, the wind that cries and sleeps and wakes again, the trees whose stiff arms clash and tremble in the dark, and the dust of lovers long since buried in the earth – all things proceeding from the earth to seasons, all things that lapse and change and come again upon the earth – these things will always be the same, for they come up from the earth that never changes, they go back into the earth that lasts forever. Only the earth endures, but it endures forever.

Now let's do a bit of rewriting, to put Wolfe's eloquent words of power into everyday English. We might come up with something like this:

> Everything on the earth always stays the same. Leaves, grass and flowers, the wind that blows and shakes trees, the buried bodies of dead lovers, the seasons of the year – these stay the same because the earth of which they are a part lasts forever.

Well, it kind of says the same things Wolfe said, but there is something missing, and that something is his personal style. His words evoke images and emotions, while the rewritten version lands in our laps with a dull plop. In Wolfe's version the wind does not merely blow, it cries, sleeps and awakes. The branches of the trees clash and tremble. It's not just their bodies but the very dust of lovers buried in the earth. There is a rhythm and flow to his words. They invoke images and emotions.

Although in the rewritten version the words are true and properly spelled and the punctuation correct and in its place, it lacks any quality of character that would compel anyone to read on to the next paragraph. While it reflects Wolfe's general ideas, it doesn't even make much if any sense.

Here is a similar example, concocted by George Orwell in his 1946 essay "Politics and the English Language." He starts with a familiar verse from Ecclesiastes, King James Edition:

> I returned and saw under the sun, that the race is not to the swift, nor the battle to the strong, neither yet bread to the wise, nor yet riches to men of understanding, nor yet favor to men of skill; but time and chance happeneth to them all.

He then presents the passage in "modern political English":

> Objective considerations of contemporary phenomena compel the conclusion that success or failure in competitive activities exhibits no tendency to be commensurate with innate capacity, but that a considerable element of the unpredictable must invariably be taken into account.

Look between the lines of any piece of fine writing and you will catch a glimpse of how personal style takes writing from the merely mundane to the exquisite, from ho-hum to oh-wow. Exquisite style is a rare and elusive thing, often sought and seldom captured. For some writers it comes easily, as fairies appear unbidden to certain cottage doors.

As E. B. White knew, style is not something to be added on to a piece of writing, like frosting on a cake. It must come from within, naturally and without effort. The focus of the author must be to tell his or her story. Effective writing does not make itself apparent but acts as a clear pane through which the reader's drawn into the imaginary world of your tale.

As the Beat Generation poet Alan Ginsberg once pointed out: "To gain your own voice, you have to forget about having it heard."

Writing in his 1985 essay *How to Write with Style*, novelist Kurt Vonnegut put it this way: "I find that I trust my own writing most, and others seem to trust it most, too, when I sound most like a person from Indianapolis, which is what I am. What alternatives do I have? The one most vehemently recommended by teachers has no doubt been pressed on you, as well: to write like cultivated Englishmen of a century or more ago."

Finding your own *voice*, and that is what personal style really is, can be the hardest thing you will ever do. Even though they come from within our own minds, our voices as writers can be so elusive that they may never be glimpsed.

As I've said in earlier chapters, I believe the art of story telling comes at least in part from our unconscious minds, those mysterious places inside our heads where all personal knowledge, thought and experience is recorded and held in readiness. That trove of secrets lies behind a curtain, revealing itself only through our dreams or – and this is key – through our writing when we have prepared our minds to let words come flowing forth as naturally and pure as a sparkling mountain stream.

It will not happen for all, or even for many, for to find your own true voice is a rare and precious thing.

Many successful writers have told of the perils to be faced along the way – the need to stand up to personal crisis; to recognize and accept often-painful self-knowledge; and to cast off the restraints of pride and walk the path of humility. It's nothing less than the process of becoming masters over the power of words. It's not unlike the cycle of birth itself, the emergence into a new and fascinating world.

Typically, to find that path we must sample the voices of others, which is why it is so important to read, to immerse ourselves in the writing of masters, and then to try on those styles for ourselves until, from the clamoring cacophony of those many voices arises that special one that is all our own.

It does not come without effort. For the young Henry Miller, it was a painful journey of self-discovery in which he was forced to renounce his very worth as a human being and cast aside everything he had done.

Here in an essay titled "Reflections on Writing," published in *The Wisdom of the Heart* (1941), he relates how he came to hear his own special voice:

> ...I imitated every style in the hope of finding the clue to the gnawing secret of how to write. Finally I came to a dead end, to a despair and desperation which few men have known, because there was no divorce between myself as writer and myself as man: to fail as a writer meant to fail as a man. And I failed. I realized that I was nothing – less than nothing – a minus quantity. It was at this point, in the midst of the dead Sargasso Sea, so to speak, that I really began to write. I began from scratch, throwing everything overboard, even those whom I most loved. Immediately I heard my own voice I was enchanted: the fact that it was a separate, distinct, unique voice sustained me. It didn't matter to me if what I wrote should be considered bad. Good and bad dropped out of my vocabulary. I jumped with two feet into the realm of aesthetics, the non-moral, non-utilitarian realm of art. My life itself became a work of art. I had found a voice, I was whole again. The experience was very much what we read of in connection with the lives of Zen initiates. My huge failure was like the recapitulation of the experience of the race: I had to grow foul with knowledge, realize the futility of every-thing, smash everything, grow desperate, then humble, then sponge myself off the slate, as it were, in order to

recover my authenticity. I had to arrive at the brink and
then take a leap in the dark.

Following are some general observations relating to style in
writing. Most of these points have been discussed in earlier
chapters, so this is a review.

• Always strive to use the fewest words possible. If a word
can be cut out, do it. Ernest Hemingway once wrote: "It
wasn't by accident that the Gettysburg address was so
short." Like all rules, this may be broken if you know what
you're doing, but your words should never create a barrier
between you and your reader.

• Use the simplest, most familiar words that best suit your
aim and fit the rhythm and flow of your work.

• Use your words to invoke imagery. As Anton Chekhov
once said: "Don't tell me the moon is shining; show me the
glint of light on broken glass."

• When possible, keep sentences short and to the point –
unless longer sentences fulfill your needs. Remember, there
are no rules.

• Never use the passive voice when it's possible to use the
active voice. (As New York Times columnist William
Safire put it as a joke: "The passive voice should never be
used.")

• Favor nouns and verbs over adjectives and adverbs.

• Seldom if ever use qualifiers such as *very, little, pretty.* If
you have chosen the right noun or verb to start with and
placed it in the proper context, no qualification should be

needed. As Mark Twain noted: "The difference between the almost right word and the right word is ... the difference between the lightning bug and the lightning."

• Avoid the temptation to use flowery language that attracts attention to itself. Samuel Johnson once advised, "Read over your compositions, and wherever you meet with a passage which you think is particularly fine, strike it out".

• Don't use meaningless words. George Orwell explained it this way: "In certain kinds of writing, particularly in art criticism and literary criticism, it is normal to come across long passages which are almost completely lacking in meaning. Words like *romantic, plastic, values, human, dead, sentimental, natural, vitality*, as used in art criticism, are strictly meaningless, in the sense that they not only do not point to any discoverable object, but are hardly ever expected to do so by the reader."

• Don't try to explain too much; let the narrative and dialog cue the reader. As Elmore Leonard advised: "Avoid detailed descriptions of characters. Same for places and things. Leave out the parts readers tend to skip."

• Avoid creating awkward adverbs, such as by adding -ly to an adjective (examples: *tiredly, thusly, overly, muchly*). Stephen King: "The road to hell is paved with adverbs."

• Don't show off by using a lot of foreign words just to show off your knowledge or for the everyday common heck of it. Few readers of English are multilingual. When foreign words are used, for example in establishing or reinforcing a character trait, they should be clearly understood from the context or explained.

• Don't use the same words or phrases too often. Repetition can grate on the nerves of readers. Hunt down echoes in your work and eliminate them.

• Beware of sentences that require too many punctuation marks. Use commas, semi-colons and dashes sparingly and for clarity. Despite what grammarians may tell you, trust me that in a simple series (example: "apples, peaches and oranges"), the word "and" serves as a comma (as would "or"). The only exception is when a comma is needed for clarification (example: "apples, peaches and cream, and oranges.") In this case the comma explains the possible confusion arising from the fact that the first "and" does not stand in for a comma.

• Use exclamation points sparingly if at all. When I ran a typesetting business, my proofreaders referred to them as "bangs," and they should be used only when that sense is appropriate, such as when something falls with a great noise, a gun is fired, a character is damning someone to hell and so forth. F. Scott Fitzgerald said of exclamation points that they are "like laughing at your own joke."

Interesting factoid: There is a typositor's character that combines an exclamation point and a question mark. It's called an "interrobang," and Merriam-Webster says it's designed for use "especially at the end of an exclamatory rhetorical question." I would not advise its use.

• Never use a metaphor, simile or other figure of speech that you have seen in common use. (An exception to this may be made in dialog, when it's appropriate to the character to be trite.)

• Finally, don't let "rules" shackle your words. As Elmore Leonard related: "If it sounds like writing, I rewrite it. Or, if proper usage gets in the way, it may have to go. I can't allow what we learned in English composition to disrupt the sound and rhythm of the narrative."

That quality we call literary style does not come easily and cannot be forced. When it has been attained it will flow naturally from the author's mind with no need for conscious summoning. Speaking at an undergraduate writing class, William Faulkner put it like this:

> "I think the story compels its own style to a great extent, that the writer don't need to bother too much about style. If he's bothering about style, then he's going to write precious emptiness – not necessarily nonsense … it'll be quite beautiful and quite pleasing to the ear, but there won't be much content in it."

When you have found your voice, when your words evoke more than just their defined meanings, you will have mastered the mystery of style. It is a quest worth pursuing, and the ultimate test of any writer.

Chapter Twelve

Wrapping It Up

Perhaps the most challenging part of writing a piece of fiction or a memoir is when you've finished your first draft. That may seem counter intuitive, but there's a reason they're called "rough" drafts, because chances are they leave a lot to be desired. *Revisions, editing, proofreading* – these are the necessary steps to be taken before a final draft is complete. And then there's the ultimate "what now?" question: How to get your precious story published. Let's take a look at these unpleasant necessities.

Writing is tough, but revisions can be tougher. The advice that in writing you must "murder your darlings" may seem harsh, but when it's time to take a critical look at your first draft it must be with the steely eye of a killer. One way to minimize the pain is to work on the finishing up while the writing is in progress. There are several ways you can do this.

> • Self-edit on the fly. When I finish roughing out a chapter, I go back and polish it before beginning the next one. This consists of making sure words are appropriate, sentences sensible, spelling correct and that the story is moving

forward. It's efficient to do this while the chapter is fresh in my mind, instead of waiting until the entire draft is done. I also look back at earlier chapters to identify plot holes and inconsistencies.

• Let reviewers see and comment on the work-in-progress. I have a small group of friends to whom I email chapters after I've done the self-editing step, asking for their input. Sometimes they catch things that I've missed, or suggest ways to improve the story. I don't always follow those suggestions, but they give me pause to consider my choices.

• Join a book club. No, not the kind that sends you books in the mail. Many towns have a group of fledgling writers who meet to discuss their work and ideas. If there's one near you, it's a good way to gain support. Find members who are willing to read your draft and provide criticism.

• Sign up for NaNoWriMo. National Novel Writing Month (November) is an online program that invites beginning writers to an effort to produce a 50,000-word novel in 30 days. In 2013 more than 300,000 people around the world participated in this program. Find out more at www.nanowrimo.org.

• Find reviewers on-line. By connecting through web sites and blogs, you can build your own network of volunteer reviewers. Many would-be writers enjoy helping others and you can win some valuable advice through the Internet. You can also learn by volunteering to review the work of others, so this can be a two-way street that benefits everyone involved.

Here's one important piece of advice: You may need to grow a thicker skin before offering your work for candid review by others. If they're doing their job, they're going to point out things that might be (gasp!) wrong with your writing. Sometimes they're right about it, too, so you should welcome this kind of critical review because it can help you become a better writer. We can always learn from our mistakes, but only if we're made aware of them, so welcome valid criticism – but take it with a grain of salt.

> Remember: when people tell you something's wrong or doesn't work for them, they are almost always right. When they tell you exactly what they think is wrong and how to fix it, they are almost always wrong. – Neil Gaiman

If you seek feedback only from those who will praise your writing without a hint of criticism, you're engaging in self-delusion. Good writing doesn't come from a committee and amateurs are poor judges of fine writing, so unless they are pros, don't take too seriously what your mother and friends have to contribute.

I once met a man at a meeting of a writer's group I belonged to who invited me to critique his novel. I took his request seriously and as a professional, so as a favor to him I read the draft and wrote a four or five page report. The story wasn't all that bad, but I saw a number of ways it could be improved and pointed these out.

The reaction was surprising. He was angry. How dare I criticize his wonderful novel! He informed me that 12 or 15 people including his mother, sisters and a brother had all read the manuscript and thought it was just superb and sure to be a best seller. He obviously wanted applause, not helpful criticism. Narcissism can be like that I guess. Taking a defensive attitude will never allow you to become a better writer, much less an excellent one. Such writers will succeed only in their own minds.

* * * *

Once the draft is complete, there are two major operations that must be done: editing and proofreading. These are not the same thing by any means (although any editor worth his salt is likely to be a pretty fair proofreader). Of course, you can wear both of those hats yourself, but unless you're really experienced in these arts I'd advise you to seek outside services.

Almost every writer can benefit from an experienced editor, someone to provide valuable guidance on how to revise their manuscripts. An editor is to a writer as a coach is to an athlete. Some writers need more help than others. An editor can help you achieve logical flow, create believable characters, write words that impact the reader, and help measure the spice and seasonings that lift a piece of writing to a higher level.

There are many freelance editors around and you can Google up a flock of them in a few minutes of keyword searching. As with anything else, be cautious about picking strangers on the web to help with your precious story.

As a general rule I advise against signing an open-ended agreement that lets them bill by the hour, since that gives them an incentive to spend more time on the work than might be necessary (and thus costing you more). A flat or per-page rate is preferred, but you shouldn't handicap your editor by being a cheapskate either. You probably shouldn't choose the editor who quotes the lowest rate, since we usually get what we pay for, but there's no need to pay a premium rate either if the candidate is qualified.

There are many levels of editing service, depending on the need. To use a clunky automotive analogy, if your manuscript is already in pretty good running condition it may just need a quick lube-and-filter job, but in the worst case an engine overhaul and new transmission may be in order. Don't let an editor sell you an overhaul if all you need is an oil change.

To leave metaphor aside, there are some options when beginning a relationship with an editor. A good starting point is to ask him or her merely to evaluate your manuscript, reading it over and providing a two or three page commentary for a reasonable fee.

I like to provide an evaluation as the first step when taking on a new editing client. It gives me the freedom to back away if the project looks to be a nightmare, and lets me give the writer some valuable general advice without a major commitment by either of us. I quote a modest flat fee for this service, which does not include reading the entire manuscript, but concentrating on the first twenty pages or so and skimming the rest to get an overall impression.

At the next level, the editor may make light changes in your work, perhaps rewriting sentences, deleting extraneous words and phrases or substituting a better word here and there, even doing some minor restructuring by moving sentences and even paragraphs around to create a smoother flow. Most editors proofread as part of the service. An editor should be able to do basic copyediting at five to ten pages an hour and might charge $30 to $40 an hour. Again, try to negotiate a flat fee or place a cap on hours.

When the manuscript really needs major work, a heavier form of editing is needed. Here the editor actually rewrites, completely revising entire passages, moving around or even deleting chapters and making other major revisions. The cost of this service is generally based on $40-50 per hour and may proceed at the rate of two to five pages per hour depending on difficulty.

One caveat when agreeing to heavy editing: Don't let editors impose their own style on your work. It's important to preserve your voice, and a good editor will recognize how to strengthen your style without corrupting its soul.

Finally, when your manuscript is in serious trouble a full-on rewrite may be required. In this case you need more than an editor, you need a ghostwriter to produce an entirely rewritten version of your story. At this stage you've probably concluded you're not cut out to be a writer, but still want to have your story told.

There's nothing wrong with that. A well-"ghosted" story is better than a clumsy pile of mismatched words that no one will ever read.

When using a ghostwriter the style doesn't matter (since there isn't much if any there) and can be that of the ghostwriter. This option is most appropriate to memoirs and is actually quite common in that genre. Standard ghostwriting fees range from twenty-five to fifty cents per word. Thus, for a forty-thousand-word memoir the cost might be in the range of $10,000-20,000. If extensive research or technical knowledge is required, the cost can be much higher. As mentioned in the Introduction, I once received $35,000 to write a non-fiction book for a corporate client, and that was more than three-and-a-half decades ago when the dollar was worth about three times more than it is today.

If you don't need editing services, an experienced proofreader can protect you from the embarrassment of misspelled words, use of the wrong ones, changing tense without good reason and so forth. Spell checking software is a wonderful tool, but lacks the ability to distinguish between the right word and a wrong one as long as the wrong one is spelled correctly. This explains the torrent of inappropriate words we often see in published work, such as writing "lead" instead of "led" as the past tense of the verb "to lead." (In that case the writers apparently believe their spelling version is pronounced like the heavy metal, and their spell checker has no clue about this.)

The cost for basic proofreading should be around two or three dollars per 250-word page. This service does not include editing beyond the correction of errors in grammar and spelling and applying consistent style (the AP Stylebook kind, not the kind that comes from your voice). The web has loads of proofreaders offering their services, and location is no problem unless you've written with Crayolas™ on large sheets of butcher paper – your electronic .doc can be emailed anywhere in the world in seconds.

Fact checking is another part of the final stage of manuscript preparation. Nothing turns a reader off quicker than mistakes that reveal the writer's ignorance. This is especially common when dealing with firearms. I often see mistakes such as confusion about whether a handgun is an automatic pistol or a revolver – sometimes the darn things seem to morph from one to the other at random as the story unfolds.

I remember a novel by a best-selling author in which a murder was committed with a shotgun firing pellets. The writer had her law enforcement characters obsessing throughout the story with the need to find the shotgun so that a lab test could prove it was the source of the pellets. I thought everyone knew that since shotguns are smooth-bore guns, their pellets can't be used to identify them; only solid bullets fired from a rifled barrel can do so.

Other times the hero or heroine is firing a semi-automatic pistol and when it runs out of ammunition it goes *click-click-click*. Well, a double action revolver can do that, but automatic pistols are repeatedly cocked by firing cartridges, so what makes them go *click* when they're empty?

There are many other areas where a little expertise can avoid embarrassing errors. In this case, a quick visit to a gun shop or firing range can provide the answers. If your story involves medical or legal facts, check with a doctor or lawyer. Take your financial questions to an accountant or banker, and questions about law enforcement to the cop that lives up the street. In any case, it's a good idea not to write extensively on subjects about which you know little or nothing.

If special knowledge plays a big part in your book, it would be a good idea to hire a fact-checker, a researcher who finds out what's right and what's not. Of course, you can do your own fact checking, and should do so to the best of your ability. I use the web to check facts as I write.

By researching as you go, you can uncover new facts to make your stories seem real. I use the Internet all the time when writing, seeking out little factoids to sprinkle into my stories. Remember that no one can know everything, but some among your readers will know about the facts you use. If you're wrong they'll be turned off, and nobody wants that.

And at last you're done, the story told – or so it may seem. But the hardest part of all may lie ahead: The ever-painful question of "getting published."

Here's the bad news: unless you're a famous person or a writer with an established track record, your chances of getting a traditional "legacy" publisher to take on your book are about the same as winning the Powerball™ drawing next Saturday.

The good news is that you can be your own publisher, thanks to something called print-on-demand (POD), and the even easier option of eBook publishing. We'll look at that below, but first I'll explain a bit about what's happened to traditional publishing.

In the "old days" publishing houses had large staffs of *readers*, usually young men and women with freshly-minted degrees in English Lit. Their jobs were to dig through the publishers' "slush piles," those stacks of manuscripts and queries submitted by would-be writers from across the world and every walk of life.

Most submissions were sent back with a form rejection note. A very few, two or three percent at most, were passed on to low level editors for a closer look. Nearly all of those, in turn, were ultimately rejected as well.

There are many stories of how successful writers first had to go through a long period of rejection. Here are some examples:

- Jack London is alleged to have papered the wall of his room with rejection slips before his first sale, collecting more than 400 of them.

- A writer of mysteries had her work repeatedly rejected for five years before landing her first sale. Her name: Agatha Christie, who went on to garner $2 billion in retail sales.

- J. K. Rowling kept a bag full of rejection slips under her bed, and her first book was only accepted when the eight-year-old daughter of a publishing executive read the manuscript of *Harry Potter and the Philosopher's Stone* and asked for more. Even then, her agent advised Rowling to get a day job because she couldn't expect to earn a living from sales of children's books. Today Rowling is one of the richest women in the world.

- Richard Bachman was advised that: "nobody will want to read a book about a seagull." *Jonathan Livingston Seagull* became the best selling novel in the U.S. two years running and eventually sold two million copies.

- Louis L'Amore received 200 rejections before his first book was published. He became Bantam's No. 1 selling author.

There are many similar stories, but perhaps the saddest is that of John Kennedy Toole whose comic novel *A Confederacy of Dunces* was rejected by major publishers. Suffering depression resulting in part from these failures, in 1969 he committed suicide at the age of 31. Some years later his mother found a publisher for the book and

Toole was posthumously awarded the Pulitzer Prize for best novel of 1981.

As you can see, getting published was never easy – but the sad truth is that it is now more difficult then ever to get accepted by a legacy publisher, and in fact virtually impossible. There are several reasons why this is true, mostly due to publishers' love of money and competition from other entertainment paths. Manuscript readers at publishing houses are mostly gone, laid off in waves of cost-cutting staff reductions.

More than ever, publishers rely heavily on established "name" authors for their bread and butter. One can hardly glance at a retail book display without seeing volumes by Stephen King, James Patterson, Brad Thor, Mary Higgins Clark, Clive Cussler, Danielle Steele, James Lee Burke, Nora Roberts, Stephen Hunter, Daniel Silva, Lee Child and other familiar names

In some instances teams of writers are put to work to produce a steady stream of work under the author's name (notably in the case of Patterson, but also others including Tom Clancy). These established writers have been transformed into word- and money-machines, cranking away to generate tons of cash for the legacy publishing companies. Unless you are already one of them – or fabulously wealthy and famous (or infamous) – your chance of gaining entrance to this exclusive club are pretty much zip to nada.

This effect can be seen most clearly in cases where the original author has given up the ghost, only to be replaced by other "ghosts" – replacement writers to keep the cash flowing for publishers and the authors' estates. Books bearing the names of Robert Ludlum, Lawrence Sanders, Ian Fleming and many others have continued to appear long after their deaths.

Following the 2013 death of Vince Flynn, author of the best-selling Mitch Rapp thrillers, it was announced that writer Kyle Mills would not only complete Flynn's last novel but write two more in the series. More recently a fourth volume in the late Stieg Larsson's *The Girl with the Dragon Tattoo* trilogy was released, with a new author. The cover is designed in the same distinctive style as the original books that became best sellers, but features the name of the new author, not Larsson's. (In fairness, I read it and it's pretty good.)

Another interesting result of this focus on established writers is that in most cases they continue to write book after book about the same characters. It used to be that writers were challenged to create entirely new novels with fresh settings and casts of characters, but now traditional publishing has followed the model of Marvel and DC comics that produce regular releases about such popular characters as Superman, Spiderman, Batman and Wonder Woman for year after year and decade after decade. Now we have whole strings of novels featuring such as Jack Reacher, Scott Horvath, Alex Cross, Dirk Pitt, Bob Lee Swagger, James Bond, Gabriel Allon and, famously, Jason Bourne. It seems it's no longer the authors themselves who are the stars, but the fictional characters they created.

With all this cost-cutting and focus on milking "name" writers and their popular characters for every last dollar, pound, euro and yen, it's easy for a beginning writer to become discouraged. But there is another path to publishing, by becoming your own publisher. Do it yourself publishing used to be an expensive proposition, but thanks to print-on-demand (POD), now you can be your own publisher with little or even no up-front expense.

To paraphrase a classic movie line: "Publishers? We don't need no steenkin' publishers."

So what is this POD thing? Well, it's based on an amazing machine that acts kind of like the Replicator on Star Trek. You put the digital files for a complete book in at one end, and out the other comes a finished book, bound with a color cover and ready to ship.

Combining Xerox digital printing technology with internal collating, binding and trimming functions, a POD machine can turn out a library quality book in a few minutes. These machines have transformed the publishing industry, giving everyone the option to become their own publisher. And no, you don't actually have to buy one of these things – there are plenty of services to print your books on demand.

In the past, to self-publish involved the expense of buying a quantity of printed books, many of which ended up sitting in garages and storage units around the world. With POD, you don't need to actually print a single book until it has a market. Amazon and many other sources use POD production to deliver books promptly and at reasonable cost.

You become a self-publisher simply by preparing your work as a digital file that a POD machine can turn into books at the touch of a keyboard button. There are hundreds of sources to help you with the process, but if you're savvy it's fairly easy to do the whole preparation job yourself. You may have to pay someone to create a cover design or help format the inside pages, but that cost is negligible compared with old-style paper-and-ink publishing. There's no inventory to buy and store so whether you sell only a few or thousands of copies doesn't matter, since you will order them up only as needed.

There are many companies that help writers to self-publish using POD. Unfortunately, I must warn you that some take advantage of writers while pretending to "help" them. Beware of any such firm that offers a variety of add-on services, for they will surely be pushing those services and charging you for them.

I know a man who got involved with such a firm and it ended up costing him nearly $15,000. In addition to preparing his books (and charging a hefty amount for each copy he ordered) they printed business cards and promo cards for his books, distributed news releases, even produced a TV commercial and ran it in a late-night time slot on some small local station in Nebraska. All of this was charged to him at premium prices, and none of it contributed anything to sales of his books.

When he told me about this, he didn't know what to do. He felt that the company "owned" his books and that they would continue to dun him for their services. I told him I thought that as soon as he expressed a desire to end the relationship they would gladly do so. Every con artist knows that when the mark is aware of what you're doing, it's time to move on. He later told me that when he emailed a request to cancel, they immediately agreed.

Not all POD publishers are like that, but you are likely to find them in surprising places. For example, once-reputable Penguin has bought up some of the worst offenders and is pushing their "services" hard. One can imagine that submissions to Penguin's slush pile are now being automatically handed off to one of those companies. Instead of paying writers for their work, they are now taking money from would-be authors who in the past would have received rejection slips.

Some of the legitimate POD publishers are Lulu, Book Locker and Amazon's CreateSpace. All of these can help you prepare your book for POD production as well as electronic versions for sale through Kindle, Nook, and a host of other on-line e-book services. Still, when dealing with a publishing service, be prepared to pay higher prices for printed books, since they make their money through markups. Such services are also likely to take a share of any sales made through Amazon or other outlets.

The best alternative may be to find a direct POD printing service and make it a truly do-it-yourself project. As mentioned above, you may need to hire an artist to design your book, but in the end you will have complete control. As an independent publisher, you can sell your books through Amazon and other outlets, setting your own prices and keeping the commissions instead of having to split them with someone else.

FYI, this and several of my other books were done with Amazon's CreateSpace, which is virtually free if you have the skills to edit, format, design and produce the finished product yourself. It's also convenient because Amazon fast-tracks your book onto their print and eBook sites.

This book is about writing, not publishing, so I won't go into the details of how to format, submit, and market your self-published work. There are many books and other resources about how to self-publish. When I selected the "books" category on Amazon.com and entered the keywords "how to self-publish", I got 1,831 results. I suggest you pick two or three such books that have four-plus star ratings and settle down to learn the ropes of publishing and promoting your book.

Well, that's all I have to say right now about how to make your fiction or memoir come to life. It's a magical art, the ability to craft with simple words of power the images, emotions, senses and excitement of an almost "real" world of imagination that springs from your mind. It's not something that comes easily, but there are many rewards for striving to become a good or even excellent writer.

Through the touch of your fingers on a keyboard, pen or pencil you can transport yourself to different times and places, create exciting characters and share adventures with them.

The writer's life is not an easy one, but devotion to the three arts of communications – speaking, reading and writing – can make your life more fully rounded, whether you reach a vast audience or merely reap the satisfaction of a job well done.

Here's one last piece of advice: Do not expect your power as a writer to come forth full-armed as Athena the goddess of wisdom and craft sprang from the forehead of Zeus. You must earn the ability to wield words of power through hard work and dedication. Take stock of yourself to decide if this is the path you want to follow. If it truly is, then pursue it as if the hounds of Hades are breathing at your back.

I'll leave you with the words of the late Isaac Asimov who produced 500 books during his career:

> A couple of months ago I had a dream, which I remember with the utmost clarity. (I don't usually remember my dreams.)
>
> I dreamed I had died and gone to Heaven. I looked about and knew where I was – green fields, fleecy clouds, perfumed air, and the distant, ravishing sound of the heavenly choir. And there was the recording angel smiling broadly at me in greeting.
>
> I said, in wonder, "Is this Heaven?"
>
> The recording angel said, "It is."
>
> I said (and on waking and remembering, I was proud of my integrity), "But there must be a mistake. I don't belong here. I'm an atheist."
>
> "No mistake," said the recording angel.
>
> "But as an atheist how can I qualify?"
>
> The recording angel said sternly, "We decide who qualifies. Not you."
>
> "I see," I said. I looked about, pondered for a moment, then turned to the recording angel and asked, "Is there a typewriter here that I can use?"
>
> The significance of the dream was clear to me. I felt Heaven to be the act of writing, and I have been in Heaven for over half a century and I have always known this.

#####

David L. Brown

Acknowledgements

My thanks to all those who contributed to the creation of this book, and especially to the following who read and commented on the manuscript: Alexandra Dell'Amore; Barbara Deputy; and Cherie Major. I also owe a great debt to those many authors who have inspired me over the years and from whom I have drawn countless insights and examples on the craft of fiction.

My very special thanks to you, my reader, from whom I welcome comments and suggestions. I invite you to visit my website at www.moabbookworks.com where you can read my further ruminations on the art of writing and learn about and order my other books. Time permitting, I am available to provide evaluation, editing and design services and can be reached by email at david@dlbrown-inc.com.